RELIGION AND
POLITICS
IN THE
SOUTH

RELIGION AND POLITICS
IN THE
SOUTH

Mass and Elite Perspectives

edited by
Tod A. Baker
Robert P. Steed
Laurence W. Moreland

PRAEGER

PRAEGER SPECIAL STUDIES • PRAEGER SCIENTIFIC

New York • Philadelphia • Eastbourne, UK
Toronto • Hong Kong • Tokyo • Sydney

Library of Congress Cataloging in Publication Data

Main entry under title:

Religion and politics in the South.

   1. Conservatism—Southern States—History—20th
century—Addresses, essays, lectures. 2. Evangelicalism—
Southern States—History—20th century—Addresses,
essays, lectures. 3. Fundamentalism—Addresses, essays
lectures. 4. Christianity and politics—Addresses, essays,
lectures. 5. Southern States—Politics and government—
1951- —Addresses, essays, lectures. 6. Political
participation—Southern States—History—20th century—
Addresses, essays, lectures. 7. Elite (Social sciences)—
Southern States—History—20th century—Addresses, essays,
lectures. I. Baker, Tod A. II. Steed, Robert P.
III. Moreland, Laurence W.
F215.R44   1983   323'.042'0975   83-21155
ISBN 0-03-069558-9 (alk. paper)

CONTENTS

ACKNOWLEDGMENTS

The central idea for this volume was generated by a series of papers presented at the third Citadel Symposium on Southern Politics held at The Citadel on March 25-27, 1982. Six of the chapters were developed largely or in part from scholarly papers presented at the conference. The remaining chapters and the Introduction were prepared especially for this volume. The symposium itself, directed by the editors of this book, was supported ably by a number of persons associated with The Citadel. Professor S. A. Arcilesi, head of the Department of Political Science, assisted with many administrative tasks involved in scheduling the conference. The Citadel's president, Maj. Gen. James A. Grimsley, Jr., and its vice-president for academic affairs, Brig. Gen. George F. Meenaghan, both have consistently supported and encouraged The Citadel Symposium on Southern Politics and have helped to develop the academic and intellectual climate necessary for such an effort to succeed. The Citadel Development Foundation provided funding for the conference, and we are particularly grateful for its continuing support and interest.

With regard to development of the manuscript, we wish to thank participants in the 1982 symposium whose suggestions and comments helped in selecting and editing the papers included in the volume. We are especially pleased that Professor Samuel S. Hill, a leading scholar on southern religion, graciously agreed to provide an introduction. Our editors and production coordinators at Praeger, especially Dorothy A. Brietbart, have smoothed and facilitated the publication process in numerous ways, and we thank them and Praeger for their valuable assistance.

Finally, we wish to express our appreciation to the many scholars on southern politics, in the South and elsewhere, who have participated in and in other ways supported The Citadel Symposium on Southern Politics.

INTRODUCTION
Samuel S. Hill

The American South is America; yet it is also the South. That truism suggests the region's continuity with the social and cultural life of the nation at large. It also points to Dixie's distinctiveness. The fact of the former, however, works to make the latter a "limited distinctiveness."[1]

Religion and politics, in addition to being the storied subjects many diplomatic people refuse to discuss, are two central aspects of the South's identity. Concerning religion, no other region in the United States—or in all of Christendom for that matter—is pervaded and dominated by Evangelical Protestantism. That impressive fact calls for some amplification (which it will receive), but even standing unexplained it points out the singularity of the region's religious life. As for politics, the phenomenon of its single-party character for three-quarters of a century following Reconstruction jolts the observer's consciousness just as much.

How could it happen that the religiously free and ethnically diverse United States could produce an entire region held under the sway of an historically minor (and mildly aberrant) family of Christianity? How could a constitutional society with such great respect for the public forum and the right of dissent generate a Democrats-only population over such a lengthy period?

In religion, the range of options has been similarly narrow. In politics, choices fell within the Democratic party—of course there have been various kinds of Democrats and policy to support. In both cases, Southerners did not acknowledge and certainly could not accredit distinctly different options, such as Roman Catholicism or liberal Protestantism in religion, or the Republican party or liberal Democrat perspectives in politics. A symbiosis between regional religion and regional politics did develop. However, the particular character of southern culture is put into the sharpest perspective when the "solid South" is seen in contrast with what is happening in the rest of the nation.

In the phrase religion and politics in the South, we have, first, an American anomaly and, second, a forceful symbiosis. The South differs from the rest of the nation; correlatively, the South has its own patterns for relating these two basic elements in society.

What has been said so far refers to the past, specifically to the long stretch from Reconstruction in the 1870s to the period of World War II and the New Deal in the 1940s. Since 1948 the voting patterns in southern locales and states have become quite complex, less predictable, and more like national patterns in terms of a two-party character. Liberal politics is not much more attractive now than it has been, although exemplars of that broad tradition appeared in various guises right through the one-party era. Populists, progressives, utopians, economic radicals, internationalists, sponsors of welfare programs, racial integrationists, and others have not been strangers to the region. Alternatives to the traditional one-party arrangement are now common, ranging from a minority of liberals to a sizable company of Republicans, some of them highly conservative. It is of course true that today's southern Republicans differ from many of yesterday's southern Democrats only at the point of endorsing the South's second party. That is to say, ideological orientation has changed little for many. Nevertheless, Southerners' enlistment in the GOP reflects a dramatic shift in regional life, which is at heart a willingness to entertain "northern," actually trans-southern, affinities. There are both an appropriateness and a significant social revisionism implicit in the growth of Republican party strength in the South during the last three decades.

What the period of the Reconstruction was to politics, the years around 1830 had already been to the South's religious life, its people, and its culture. About that time, the family of Evangelical Protestantism climbed into the saddle to stay.[2] Previously, during the colonial period the English pattern of an established church had prevailed—though without much success. That was followed by a transitional third-of-a-century in which it was unclear whether the region would be pervasively religious or which groups would be most prominent. But Baptist and Methodist advances, Presbyterian anchorage, and emergence of the indigenously American Campbellite movement sealed the future. Perhaps it is useful to describe Methodism as the center of gravity, with Baptist energy as the generating force, and Presbyterianism as the traditionalist boundary that afforded some stability and prevented excesses in Catholic directions.

Some new blood was pumped into the southern "body religious" before and after the turn of the present century, but it provided more of the same; that is, "excesses" in the other direction, toward a more intense and demonstrative Evangelicalism. These Holiness, Pentecostal, and Fundamentalist groups variously sought to restore and activate the original purity and spiritedness of earlier forms of Evangelicalism. They intended to introduce nothing new and their intentions were fulfilled. They did enlarge the spectrum of social classes and types of communities in which vital religion functioned, but the Evangelical drift of traditional regional religion was perpetuated nevertheless.

The South was largely impervious to foreign invasions in both religion and politics during the period from Reconstruction to the 1940s.

Moreover the rhythms of regional culture were rather regular and stable. Out of this cultural context there developed a predictable arrangement between the two elements in southern society. Religion and politics acquired rather set places in the people's minds and in the regional mythos. Religion came to mean church and theology, the agency responsible for taking care of life's spiritual and eternal aspects and for providing "good people" for all walks of life, including the political and public. Politics was understood as operating by its own objectives and standards, sticking to its own area, and borrowing little directly from religion or making little direct impact on it. It was left to the Presbyterians to provide the phrase, "the spirituality of the church," in describing the culturally approved role of religion. [3] But that view of the relation between church and government was conventional wisdom. Only idiosyncratic individuals departed from it.

One must understand that the religious practitioners of the "religion and politics don't mix" mentality were not radical sectarians—that is, people on the edges of society's mainstream—or fringe groups hostile to it. People in the major white denominations were and still are that mainstream. As a matter of fact, until quite recently success in being elected to public office virtually required membership in an acceptable church. Even so, religion and politics are understood as separate and nonoverlapping arenas. The former produces the "good Christians" who hold office in the latter; it also inculcates the values that are essential for a healthy society.

Against this backdrop the recent appearance of the Moral Majority, Inc.—in fact, the entire new religious-political Right (NRPR) in America—is richly illuminating. In the first place it must be noted that this movement is not notably southern, despite many popular assumptions. Its most visible leader, Jerry Falwell, is a Southerner to be sure, but his is an independent Baptist tradition and, more significantly, the members of Moral Majority are not primarily southern. Upper South states are moderately well represented in the membership, but Deep South areas are not. Moreover, the Midwest and southern California are areas of strength for this religious-political cause attracting the loyalty of a few million people many of whom are moral-political conservatives without deep religious commitments and convictions.

Second, the degree and nature of political participation by these Evangelicals—who are of the Fundamentalist subset within that family, by the way—are most unusual within the southern religious setting. It is even more unusual behavior for Fundamentalists, no matter where in the country they are to be found. The NRPR movement is diverging from regional norms and customs. As has been noted, southern Christians generally have not involved themselves directly as Christians in the political process. They have not seen it as their business to back candidates, to campaign for causes (with a few exceptions such as prohibition), and to organize drives to get people to vote. And the more conservative—that is, the closer to Fundamentalist—they have been, the greater has been their aversion to direct political activity.

Thus Jerry Falwell, Moral Majority, and other NRPR supporters in the South, though not quite alien, are anomalous. They serve to confirm the "religion and politics don't mix" tradition of the region. The position they take does not fit. It has received the formal approval of no denomination, no matter how conservative. While some of their views and concerns are widely held among southern Christians, the total package is rejected. One suspects that its lack of congruity with southern religious and religious-political conventions is a major factor. [4]

The principal conclusion from this line of analysis is that religion and politics in the South is a specific tradition that must be carefully examined through the kinds of scrutiny reflected in this book. It cannot be stereotyped. It is not Fundamentalist. It is far removed from the posture of radical sectarianism. It does not allow precise identifiability through organizations, such as Moral Majority, that have specific, positive programs. In terms of historic Christian patterns, it does not differ significantly less from the Reformation notions of Luther and Calvin than from medieval Catholicism. Nor does it resemble the Anabaptist theory of separation and deliberate shunning of public affairs and institutions. It is the South's singular tradition and must be understood as such. While hardly unprecedented and having some connections with other patterns, it is indeed the South's own; it derives more from the theology and methods of revivalism than from any rationalized interpretation of the proper relationship between church and state. As its base, the southern tradition has affinity with Calvinism in its conviction that religion and politics are partners in maintaining or creating a godly society, but it strikes its own course in seeing the religious role and achievements of the political sphere as indirect and epiphenomenal. In its heart of hearts, so to speak, southern religion puts its stock in the personal piety of converted individuals whose lives reflect biblical righteousness in daily behavior. [5]

Lest the point has been made to excess and therefore is misleading, however, one needs to keep clear that religion and politics have been related, never mind theory or intentions. Three recent studies of great importance establish that correlation quite vividly.

In 1977 Donald G. Mathews published Religion and the Old South in which he argued, among other conclusions, that the Evangelical religion of the antebellum South produced direct political results. [6] While individualistic in its focus on personal salvation, it called for the disciplined and righteous life of Christians aspiring to perfection. It thus created people and a society much taken with general holiness. They believed that God willed for them to be bound together in building his kingdom on earth through spiritual churches, ideal families, good educational institutions, constructive relations between masters and slaves, and a godly public order. Thus, although the slated goals of church life left out the Christianizing of society in its corporate aspects, they produced values and activities that overflowed the banks of church life and made their mark on public life.

The second book to be noted is Baptized in Blood: The Religion of the Lost Cause, 1865-1920 by Charles Reagan Wilson.[7] This study points out that the mythos of the Lost Cause—the glorification of a civilization brought down by war—was accorded a transcendent status and given public expression. Confederate heroes and Old South values were not simply remembered and revered; their recollection was perpetuated in statues, cemeteries, colleges, and rituals. The Lost Cause was not treated merely as spirituality; its memory was preserved through public expressions, many of them directly political. One of its effects was the consolidation of all things southern, including the Democratic party, in the face of incursions from beyond or alternative arrangements for cultural life. Southern society attained its greatest homogeneity in that era.

The Pulitzer Prize-winning book for history in 1983 was Rhys Isaac's The Transformation of Virginia, 1740-1790.[8] It dramatically demonstrates the correlation between religion and politics—indeed, between church and society—during the decades of transition between colonial Virginia and statehood. The impact of religion and politics was mutual and reciprocal, with the dismantling of old social hierarchies feeding the democratic spirit of Baptist and Methodist piety, and with those popular churches serving to give vent to resentments against people of high standing and authoritarian position. At all events, religion was up to its steeples in both the political and general social life of late colonial Virginia, and emergent republicanism was nurtured by Evangelical denominations that bowed before no superiors and lived by a spirituality that was no respecter of persons.

The South definitely has followed its own course. This can be seen as clearly through the three period-specific books described above as through observation of the sweep of southern history. Even though changes have occurred since the 1940s, regional distinctiveness continues. The voting behavior and political causes of the black population contribute to the patterns of change, both as a new outlook and as occasion for reaction by some southern whites. But this item on the change page of the ledger must be written on the continuity sheet as well, because the coexistence of black people and white people has always been a dominant factor in southern life. Only the nature of the interaction has been altered.

The studies collected in this book promise to advance an understanding of the South, its religion, its politics, and the distinctive ways in which they are interrelated in the region. A topic hitherto insufficiently studied, religion and politics in the South may be coming into its own as a field of critically important inquiry.

NOTES

1. This term was coined and developed in Carl N. Degler, Place over Time (Baton Rouge: Louisiana State University Press, 1977).

2. See Samuel S. Hill, Southern Churches in Crisis (New York: Holt, Rinehart & Winston, 1966), especially chap. 4.

3. See Ernest Trice Thompson, Presbyterians in the South (Richmond, Va.: John Knox Press, 1973), especially vols. 2 and 3.

4. See Samuel S. Hill and Dennis E. Owen, The New Religious-Political Right in America (Nashville, Tenn.: Abingdon Press, 1982), chaps. 2 and 8.

5. Hill, Southern Churches in Crisis, chaps. 5 and 6.

6. Donald G. Mathews, Religion and the Old South (Chicago: University of Chicago Press, 1977).

7. Charles Reagan Wilson, Baptized in Blood: The Religion of the Lost Cause, 1865–1920 (Athens: University of Georgia Press, 1980).

8. Rhys Isaac, The Transformation of Virginia, 1740–1790 (Chapel Hill: University of North Carolina Press, 1982).

PART I

SOUTHERN POLITICS AND RELIGION: MASS PERSPECTIVES

INTRODUCTION TO PART I

In a democracy public policy is presumably formulated within the set of constraints imposed by the attitudes, beliefs, and values of the mass of the citizenry. [1] In short, culture—or more specifically, political culture—tends to serve as a set of constraints, and consequently, an understanding of mass political orientations is important in studying the political system.

This volume broadly examines the relationship between religious beliefs and political attitudes and behavior in a region that has created and maintained a rather distinct subcultural identity. [2] Furthermore, since Southerners have historically tended to take religion quite seriously, religious beliefs and practices have constituted a rather important subcultural trait. [3]

The chapters in Part I focus on various connections between religion and politics within the southern electorate. In Chapter 1 Michael Mezey analyzes survey data collected between 1972 and 1980 by the National Opinion Research Center in an effort to identify attitudes that distinguish the South from the remainder of the nation. In doing this he is able, among other things, to examine certain religious perspectives within a broader configuration of attitudes on a range of issues. In turn, this helps to place southern religious attitudes in a wider attitudinal context.

In Chapter 2 Corwin Smidt compares southern and nonsouthern Evangelicals in terms of their social characteristics, issue orientations, politicization, and partisanship. Smidt's analysis is based on data drawn from the 1980 presidential election study conducted by the Center for Political Studies at the University of Michigan. The South is defined as the Confederate states minus Tennessee, and Evangelicals are defined as those who state that religion plays an important part in their lives, who have a literal belief in the Bible, and who report having had a "born-again" experience.

On the other hand, in Chapter 3 Jerry Perkins, Donald Fairchild, and Murray Havens compare the attitudes and behavior of Evangelical and non-Evangelical Southerners on the basis of race. The topics addressed largely parallel those covered by Smidt. Perkins, Fairchild, and Havens also base their analysis on the 1980 Center for Political Studies presidential election study, but their definition of Evangelical differs somewhat from that employed by Smidt. For Perkins and his colleagues, an Evangelical is one who says that religion is important to one's life, that it offers quite a bit or a great deal of guidance, that one has been born again, and that the Bible is literally the word of God.

Finally, in Chapter 4 Kenneth Wald and Michael Lupfer seek to determine the causal role of religious belief. Their analysis is based on a sample drawn from residents of the Memphis Standard Metropolitan Statistical Area in 1981. Although these authors develop a 14-point measure of religious orthodoxy as opposed to Evangelicalism, their measure at least appears to have a great deal of congruence with the concept of Evangelicalism as used in the previous two chapters.

Although these four chapters employ a diverse set of data, techniques, and definitional considerations, their conclusions and related discussions are generally consistent, at least in instances where their mutual concerns overlap. In other instances the discussions are quite complementary. Collectively they do much to advance an understanding of the religious factor within the southern electorate, specifically, and within the region's political arena, generally.

NOTES

1. There are a number of excellent treatments of public opinion and political behavior within a democratic political system. Among others, see V. O. Key, Jr., Public Opinion and American Democracy (New York: Alfred A. Knopf, 1961); and Dennis S. Ippolito and Thomas G. Walker, Political Parties, Interest Groups, and Public Policy: Group Influence in American Politics (Englewood Cliffs, N.J.: Prentice-Hall, 1980), especially chap. 1.

2. See, for example, Numan V. Bartley, "The South and Sectionalism in Southern Politics," Journal of Politics 38 (August 1976): 257.

3. Note the discussion in John Shelton Reed, The Enduring South: Subcultural Persistence in a Mass Society (Lexington, Mass.: D. C. Heath, Lexington Books, 1972).

1

THE MINDS
OF THE SOUTH

Michael L. Mezey

One of the continuing questions for students of southern society and its politics—for some, the only question—has been whether or not the South is different or distinct from the rest of the United States in terms of its prevailing customs and politics. This discussion has proceeded from the premise that at one time the South was clearly different, but that more recently forces have been at work to erode this distinctiveness with the result that southern politics and culture have begun to converge with the politics and culture of the nation as a whole. Among the dimensions of change that have been discussed are the political and social attitudes of Southerners, the nature of southern voting behavior, and the behavior and attitudes of southern politicians at home and in Washington, D. C. [1]

This chapter is concerned with attitudes. More specifically, it tries to determine whether or not a distinction continues between southern attitudes and those of the rest of the country, on what particular issues this distinction is most apparent, and whether or not the distinction is more or less apparent among different demographic groups. The attitudes to be examined will not be restricted to traditional political variables such as party identification and liberalism-conservatism scales, but will include as well the broader pattern of social and cultural attitudes that are the antecedents of those beliefs usually thought of as political. [2]

The literature bearing on the nature of southern distinctiveness comes to somewhat different conclusions. Working primarily with data from the 1950s and 1960s, John Shelton Reed and Norval Glenn found an enduring distinctiveness in southern attitudes. [3] Ted Jelen, writing more recently, demonstrated a particularly strong distinction on the issue of tolerance, which he attributed largely to southern religious beliefs. [4] In contrast, Earl Hawkey concluded that on a general liberal-conservative dimension as well as on several specific policy issues, there has been a general pattern of convergence.[5] This view is supported by Norman R. Luttbeg and Robert S. Erikson who also found evidence of convergence on economic issues, although marked divergence on noneconomic issues, particularly race and tolerance, persists.[6] This conclusion is shared by Jack Bass and Walter De-Vries who believe that the differences between South and non-South are fading and that on many issues the differences between southern blacks and southern whites exceed the differences between southern and nonsouthern whites. However, they also found that there are some issues—especially those involving religion—that do continue to separate Southerners from non-Southerners.[7]

The suggestion that there may be at least two southern belief systems—one white and one black—can be readily extended to other demographic variables. If the unique nature of southern attitudes was shaped originally by a relatively homogeneous, primarily rural society characterized by comparatively low income, then it is reasonable to believe that the well-documented phenomena of increased urbanism and expanding industry might divide Southerners into different attitudinal groups and might produce belief systems differentiated by more than race.[8]

For example, on certain issues conflict may be class based as poor whites and poor blacks unite in common cause against the more privileged. Another possibility is that the South will move toward two distinct cultures, one representing the more modernized urban sector and the other representing the more traditional rural society. In this scenario, conflict in the South will come to resemble the pattern of many northern states where urban and suburban interests frequently stand opposed to rural interests.

Clearly, neither race nor socioeconomic status nor urbanism can be expected to define completely the parameters of conflict on all issues. Rather, a specific demographic factor may explain a good portion of the variance on one issue but very little on another, or on certain issues more than one factor may be important. It is also possible that there may yet still be something of a regional consensus transcending demographic differences on certain issues. In sum, this perspective emphasizes southern diversity rather than homogeneity and suggests that rather than one mind of the South there are likely to be many minds of the South, some more and some less distinctive from the minds of other Americans.[9]

The strategy for investigating these possibilities involves three stages. First is an examination of a wide range of issues to determine the extent to which regionalism can explain variance in attitudes. Second, the attitudes of particular population groups will be explored to determine whether or not regional distinctions are more salient for some population sectors than for others. Third, the attitudes of Southerners will be reviewed to determine which demographic variables divide Southerners from each other.

WHAT ARE SOUTHERN BELIEFS?

On what issues can southern attitudes be expected to be distinct and what direction is that distinction likely to take? In some cases, distinctiveness has been documented in the empirical literature on southern politics and culture. Sometimes, expectations of distinctiveness are based on the more impressionistic discussions of the South and its people found in the memoirs of journalists and in the fiction of southern writers. Finally, some expectations are based on little more than current conventional wisdom or on more or less disciplined observations of the behavior of southern political elites. Given these multiple sources of expectations, it should not be surprising to find often conflicting views of what southern attitudes should look like.

Perhaps the greatest consensus is on the word conservative as a description of southern attitudes. When John Shelton Reed asked college students to select typically southern traits from a list of 84 choices, the leading choice was conservative, closely followed by the related term, tradition-loving. [10] Of course, as every veteran of an introductory political science course knows, the term conservative is not one for which there is a definitional consensus.

For example, the term conservative is often used to describe southern religious beliefs, the nature of which is treated in several other chapters in this volume. As these discussions suggest, religion in the South, particularly its dominant Protestant faiths, has been "characterized by high visibility, conservatism, and emotionalism." [11] Reed cited conservative religious beliefs as one of the defining characteristics of "the enduring South," and authors before and since his work have attested to the centrality of religious Fundamentalism and Evangelicalism to the culture of the white South. [12] Similarly, the importance of religion to the culture of the black South has been well documented. [13]

Closely related to religious beliefs in Reed's analysis are conservative attitudes toward the family. [14] Based on this perspective, one would expect to find support in the South for traditional values that eschew sexual permissiveness, elevate respect for elders, and place women in the home and subordinate to their husbands. [15] Thus, although William J. Cash writes of the "cult of southern womanhood," there is also some evidence to the contrary. [16] Hawkey finds little difference between northern and southern attitudes on women's rights. [17] Cash, although noting southern adherence to traditional values, also speaks of a tradition of hedonism in southern culture that contrasts with the puritanical terms often used to describe the southern moral code. [18]

Another, perhaps more conventional, aspect of conservatism involves attitudes toward economic issues and a resistance to government, particularly to government programs that are perceived to be aimed at redistributing the wealth and otherwise interfering with the lives of citizens. This set of attitudes presumably is based on individualism, which according to Cash is the dominant trait of the southern mind. [19] While the voting records of southern members of Congress may suggest that economic conservatism continues to be the hallmark of the South, it also has been noted that southern political attitudes are not as conservative as the behavior of southern political leaders. [20] Furthermore, as William Havard reminds us, the history of populism in the South implies greater support for economic liberalism than the conventional wisdom suggests, a view most recently supported by data that Hawkey has assembled. [21]

A third dimension of conservatism involves a posture toward the nation's relationship with the rest of the world. Currently, this view incorporates greater support for the armed forces and for defense spending and a more narrow and hostile view of communism and the Soviet Union than might be exhibited in other parts of the country. The basis for expecting these attitudes to characterize the South lies both in the region's traditionally favorable view of the military and use of military force and in the behavior of many southern politicians in Washington, D.C., who seem to be among our more consistent cold warriors. [22] In addition, as Cash suggests, the religiosity of the South made the region particularly antagonistic toward "atheistic" communism. [23]

If southern leaders have been hostile to forces of disorder abroad, they also have exhibited conservative attitudes toward disorder at home. Law and order conservatism thus may be more apparent in the South than in the rest of the country, a view seemingly substantiated by Hawkey's data. [24] In this connection, it is ironic to note the role of violence as one of the hallmarks of what Reed calls the enduring South. [25] This, it has been argued, has led to the high incidence of gun ownership in the South and to the strong resistance there to gun control legislation.

The contradictions apparent within the expected southern attitude structure are also evident in regard to southern attitudes toward outsiders. While southern hospitality and friendliness have been among the more widely advertised traits of the region, Bass and DeVries note a tradition of deep hostility toward and suspicion of outsiders. [26] Similarly, Jelen documents a still pervasive intolerance in the South toward people who are perceived to be different. [27] One wonders, therefore, how Southerners view their world—as a friendly place where people can be liked and trusted or as a hostile world in which one must always be on one's guard. Part of this view is influenced by and reflected in the degree to which people are satisfied with their lives. Again, there are contradictions. The slow pace of southern life, the congenial climate, and the lower cost of living would lead one to think that Southerners as a group must be happier and more content with their lives than people who live in regions of the country where daily life is more contentious. On the other hand, the prosperity of the Sun Belt, the relative poverty of some areas that have not yet been caught up in this boom, the generally poor state of many public services, the tradition of violence and intolerance, and—for blacks at least—overt racial hostility suggest that life may not be as pleasant in the South as in other places. [28]

This last point leads to the topic of racial attitudes, which historically, constitute the cornerstone of southern distinctiveness. This is not the place to examine the nature and history of racism in the South, but clearly these attitudes more than any other have distinguished the South from other regions of the country. However, in the last 15 years the 1965 Voting Rights Act has enfranchised southern blacks, some of the more retrograde racist practices have been ameliorated, and most significantly, race has become as tendentious an issue outside the South as within it. These factors suggest at least a decline in southern distinctiveness on questions of race because whites, both northern and southern, have changed their views.

DATA

The foregoing discussion has alluded to several attitudinal areas. These may be grouped into the following 11 categories: religion, moral issues, women's roles, economic issues, tolerance, violence, law and order, national defense and communism, interpersonal trust, satisfaction with life, and race. The data presented in this chapter come from questions included in the General Social Surveys administered by the National Opinion Research Center between 1972 and 1980. [29] For most items, data are pooled from several different years within the period. This has the advantage of providing a large number of cases, thereby facilitating analyses using several control variables. It also has the advantage of reducing the impact of short-term forces on the results. The major drawback, however, is that the approach obscures and therefore ignores attitudinal changes that undoubtedly took place in the eight years between the 1972 surveys and those taken in 1980.

HOW DISTINCTIVE IS THE SOUTH?

In order to determine the degree to which the South continues to be distinctive in the 11 issue areas, 47 variables, consisting of single questionnaire items and scales combining several items, were each subjected to a four-way analysis of variance using region, urbanism, race, and income as independent variables. The items are displayed in Table 1.1 along with two statistics generated by a multiple-classification analysis. The eta coefficient assesses the explanatory power of region without controlling for other independent variables. This is equivalent to the measures of southern distinctiveness frequently seen in the daily press when national survey results are simply cross-tabulated on the basis of region. The second statistic, beta, measures the effect of region after controlling for the effects of the other three independent variables. This is a more accurate indicator of southern distinctiveness because it filters out the possibility that differences between the South and the rest of the nation on a particular issue arise from factors such as relatively low family income in the region, large numbers of blacks in the population, or a high percentage of rural dwellers.[30]

The issue areas are arranged in Table 1.1 with topics listed first on which southern distinctiveness is most pronounced. In nearly every case the southern responses are in the predicted direction, although the magnitude of the distinction varies markedly across issue areas. When the attitudes of white respondents only are assessed, racial issues most sharply delineate the South from the rest of the nation.[31] Particularly salient are attitudes toward social relations between blacks and whites and toward school and housing integration. However, it also should be noted that regional distinctions are very small on issues such as busing and affirmative action, suggesting that the rest of the nation has been no more enthusiastic about these policies than the South has been.

A second area of obvious southern distinctiveness involves items measuring tolerance of the rights of atheists, communists, and homosexuals to speak in the community, teach in colleges, and have books advocating their preferences in the public library. These data replicate Jelen's finding that "the South still retains a distinctive regional character regarding tolerance toward nonconformists."[32] Somewhat less regionally divisive than race or tolerance, but still areas in which the South is clearly different, are attitudes toward the military and sense of interpersonal trust. Southerners are more disposed than other Americans to support high levels of military spending and to articulate great confidence in the military establishment. In regard to interpersonal trust, they are more likely than non-Southerners to feel that people will try to take advantage of them and that most people are looking out for themselves.

TABLE 1.1

Regional Distinctions

Item (variable name)	Southern Response	Eta	Beta	(N)
Race relations				
1. Attitudes toward integrating suburbs, interracial marriage, and desirability of black supervisors for white workers (RACE-1)	Against	.13	.17	(1,334)
2. Attitudes toward interracial marriage, interracial social gatherings, housing and school integration, and voting for a black for president (white respondents only, RACE-2)	Against	.28	.24	(4,033)
3. Why blacks have worse jobs, income, and housing than whites (white respondents only, RACE-3)	Less ability, less motivation	.15	.15	(1,179)
4. Government in Washington, D.C., should help blacks/minorities to improve their position, even if it means giving them preferential treatment (HLPMINR)	Against	.02	.04	(1,361)
5. Busing of schoolchildren (BUSING)	Against	.02	.07	(8,761)

(continued)

11

TABLE 1.1 (continued)

Item (variable name)	Southern Response	Eta	Beta	(N)
Tolerance				
6. Toward atheists (ATHTOL)	Intolerant	.20	.15	(8,563)
7. Toward Communists (COMTOL)	Intolerant	.17	.13	(8,305)
8. Toward homosexuals (HOMOTOL)	Intolerant	.19	.15	(6,950)
The military and communism				
9. Attitude toward increasing defense spending (DEFSPDR)	For	.13	.13	(1,303)
10. Attitude toward current spending on military, armaments, and defense (NATARMS)	Too little	.12	.12	(9,747)
11. Confidence in the people running the military (CONARMY)	A great deal	.11	.10	(10,062)
12. Attitude toward Soviet Union (RUSSIA)	Dislike	.10	.09	(4,210)
13. Attitude toward communism as a form of government (COMMUN)	Worst kind of all	.09	.08	(7,253)
14. Do people try to be helpful?	No			
Do people try to take advantage of you?	Yes	.13	.10	(8,194)
Can most people be trusted? (PERTRUST)	No			

13

Moral issues

15. Attitude toward premarital sex (PREMARSX)	Always wrong	.16	.15	(7,339)
16. Attitude toward sexual relations, adults of same sex (HOMOSEX)	Always wrong	.14	.10	(7,046)
17. Attitude toward sex education in public schools (SEXEDUC)	Against	.10	.07	(4,345)
18. Should the use of marijuana be made legal? (GRASS)	Should not	.10	.08	(7,209)
19. Younger generation should be taught by their elders or taught to think for themselves, even though they may do something their elders disapprove of (YOUNGEN)	Taught by elders	.09	.08	(1,455)
20. Attitude toward adultery (XMARSEX)	Always wrong	.09	.07	(7,373)
21. Should birth control information be available to teen-agers? (TEENPILL)	Should not	.06	.04	(4,366)
22. Should birth control information be available to anyone? (PILL)	Should not	.05	.03	(4,424)
23. Attitude toward pornography laws (PORNLAW)	For	.05	.04	(7,347)
24. Attitude toward divorce law change (DIVLAW)	Made more difficult	.03	.02	(7,127)

Women's rights

25. Attitudes toward women having careers, women being involved in politics, and voting for a female candidate for president (FEM-1)	Against	.12	.09	(5,884)
26. Attitudes toward relationship between working women and children, between wives and husbands, and toward ERA (FEM-2)	Disapprove	.10	.07	(1,502)
27. Attitude toward abortion (ABORTSUM)	Against	.09	.06	(11,787)

(continued)

TABLE 1.1 (continued)

Item (variable name)	Southern Response	Eta	Beta	(N)
Religion				
28. Attitude toward Supreme Court ruling forbidding states to require reading of Bible or Lord's Prayer in schools (PRAYER)	Disapprove	.13	.11	(3,660)
29. Frequency of attendance at religious services (ATTEND)	Frequently	.10	.09	(12,033)
30. Strength of religious commitment (RELITEN)	Strong	.06	.04	(8,213)
31. Confidence in the people running organized religion (CONCLERG)	A great deal	.01	.01	(9,997)
Violence				
32. Attitude toward law requiring police permit to buy gun (GUNLAW)	Oppose	.09	.08	(10,322)
33. Do you or spouse go hunting? (HUNT)	Yes	.08	.07	(2,990)
34. Are there situations in which you would approve of a man punching an adult male stranger? (HITOK)	Yes	.00	.02	(7,176)
Quality of life				
35. How much satisfaction do you get from the city or place you live in? (SATCITY)	A great deal	.07	.07	(10,461)

14

No.	Question	Response			N
36.	How satisfied are you with the work that you do? (SATJOB)	Very satisfied	.05	.06	(9,419)
37.	How happy would you say you are? (HAPPY)	Very happy	.03	.05	(12,043)
38.	How satisfied are you with your present financial situation? (SATFIN)	Pretty well satisfied	.01	.03	(12,035)

Economic/government issues

No.	Question	Response			N
39.	Attitude toward government spending to improve and protect the environment and the nation's health, to solve problems of big cities, to improve the educational system and the condition of blacks (NATSUM)	Spending too much	.03	.04	(9,664)
40.	Attitude toward government in Washington, D.C., reducing income differences between rich and poor (EQWLTH)	Opposed	.00	.04	(3,911)
41.	Confidence in people running banks and financial institutions (CONFINAN)	A great deal	.04	.03	(7,321)
42.	Confidence in people running major companies (CONBUS)	A great deal	.01	.03	(9,947)
43.	Confidence in people running the executive branch of the federal government, the U.S. Supreme Court, and the Congress (CONPUB)	A great deal	.02	.02	(9,742)
44.	Attitude toward government providing fewer services, even in areas such as health and education, in order to reduce spending (CUTSPDR)	Oppose	.01	.01	(1,308)

Law and order

No.	Question	Response			N
45.	Do you favor or oppose the death penalty? (CAPPUN)	Oppose	.03	.00	(8,444)
46.	Do courts deal too harshly or not harshly enough with criminals? (COURTS)	Too harshly	.02	.00	(10,509)

Source: Compiled by the author from National Opinion Research Center data.

15

Attitudes on moral issues vary in regard to regional influence. Some items, such as attitudes toward premarital sex and homosexuality, display distinctions of great magnitude between the South and the rest of the nation. In contrast, attitudes toward laws dealing with pornography, divorce, and birth control are less regionally divisive. Women's rights issues tend to fall between these two extremes, with the South, as predicted, somewhat more conservative than the rest of the nation.

While attitudes on religion and violence, which Reed thought to be the most enduring southern traits, continue to divide the South from other regions, those items taken as a whole do not display the same level of regional distinctiveness as the issue areas already mentioned. Again, there is variation across the items with attitudes toward prayer in the public schools showing a great deal of southern distinctiveness, while confidence in the clergy shows no southern distinctiveness at all. Similarly, perceptions of the quality of life are relatively higher in the South on the community satisfaction item, but much less distinctive on the item dealing with satisfaction with one's personal financial situation.

At the bottom of the list are attitudes toward economic issues; these data seem to match earlier findings that virtually none of the nationwide variance on issues of this sort can be attributed to regionalism. It is particularly interesting to note that despite the presumed southern commitment to individualism and suspicion of government in Washington, D.C., confidence in national political institutions is in fact slightly higher in the South. Finally, contrary to Hawkey's findings, these data show no southern distinctiveness on the two law and order issues included in this analysis.

In brief, then, the answer to the question of whether or not the South is distinct from the rest of the nation depends on what issues are being discussed. On some, such as race, tolerance, and national defense, the answer is clearly yes. On others, such as economic conservatism and law and order, the answer is definitely no. On the new social issues associated with religion, morality, tolerance, the role of women, and quality of life, the answer is sometimes.

WHICH SEGMENT OF THE SOUTH IS MOST DISTINCTIVE?

Although attitudes in the South have been changing, there is no reason to think the entire South has experienced the same degree of change. It is more likely that there are segments of the southern population whose attitudes are less distinct from those of other Americans, while for other Southerners the distinctions will be a good deal more pronounced.

To test for this variation, the national population sample was divided into nine demographic groups by combining racial, urban, and socioeconomic categories. This produced three white urban groups and three white rural groups differentiated by income level, one black urban low-income group, one black urban medium- to upper-income group, and one black rural group not subdivided by income level. Distinctions between southern and nonsouthern respondents within each of these nine groups were examined across various questionnaire items and scales. The results are summarized in Table 1.2. The plus signs in Table 1.2 indicate a relatively high degree of distinction between the northern and southern components of the groups; the minus signs indicate very little regional distinction. In most cases, percent differences in responses were averaged across several items within an issue area in order to simplify the presentation. Note that the entries in Table 1.2 do not indicate a direction to the distinction; that is, a plus sign does not indicate that the southern group is more or less conservative than the northern group. The sign simply indicates the magnitude of the distinction between the northern and southern respondents.

Although the pattern in Table 1.2 is not always consistent, some tendencies are fairly obvious. For one, the white rural portion of the population—especially the very poor and the very well-off—shows the most consistently large distinctions between northern and southern respondents. Conversely, there is a tendency for southern white urbanites, regardless of income level, to be most proximate in their view to their counterparts in northern urban areas. On issues where the overall distinctions between South and non-South are greatest—race, interpersonal trust, the military, feminism, tolerance, morality, and religion—the tendency is toward greater regional distinctions between white rural respondents and minor regional distinctions between white urban respondents. On issues where overall distinctions are smallest—satisfaction with life, economic conservatism, and law and order—the southern white rural respondents are also generally indistinguishable from their northern counterparts. Perhaps the obvious conclusion is that the bedrock of southern distinctiveness is found in the white rural South and that regional distinctions are diminishing in the white urban South.

The data in Table 1.2 also show a pattern of clear distinctions between southern and northern blacks, especially on issues such as abortion, national defense, religion, law and order, and satisfaction with life. The southern black respondents most proximate to their northern counterparts are middle-income urbanites, but even for this group large distinctions are as frequent as minor distinctions. The data should reinforce the point that southern black culture is distinct from northern black culture and that, contrary to simplistic notions,

TABLE 1.2

Southern Distinctiveness by Population Group and Issue Area

Issue Area	White Urban			White Rural			Black Urban		Black Rural
	Low Income	Middle Income	High Income	Low Income	Middle Income	High Income	Low Income	Middle and High Income	
Race	−		−	+		+		−	−
Tolerance		−	−	+	+	+	−		+
Military		−	−	+	+		+	+	+
Trust		−	−	+	+		−	+	
Abortion	−	−	−			−	+	+	+
Women's rights	−	+		+	+	+			
Morality	−	−		+	−	+	−		+
Religion					+	+		+	+
Violence	+	−	+	−	−	+	−	−	+
Quality of life	+		−		−	−	+		+
Economics	−	+	+		−	+		−	
Law and order	−			−	−		+	+	+

Note: + means relatively large distinction between southern and nonsouthern portions of the population group;
− means relatively small distinction between southern and nonsouthern portions of the population group.

Source: Compiled by the author from National Opinion Research Center data.

the communities cannot be expected to respond to issues in the same way.[33]

WHAT ACCOUNTS FOR DIFFERENCES
WITHIN THE SOUTH?

It should be clear to this point that the South cannot be viewed as a homogeneous unit when comparisons are drawn between it and the rest of the nation. To get a better understanding of the nature of conflict in the South, a separate analysis of variance was run for each item and scale for the southern portion of the sample presented in the previous section. Race, urbanism, and income were used as independent variables. Results of the multiple classification analysis are shown in Table 1.3. The coefficients, which are betas, indicate the explanatory power of each of the independent variables with the effects of the other two variables controlled.

Race. Southern respondents divide along racial lines on some quite predictable issues. Of course, blacks have different views from whites on racial issues; also, they are more disposed toward economic liberalism, less disposed toward the culture of violence, and more liberal on law and order issues. These findings are not very surprising given the extreme economic inequalities between blacks and whites in the South and the fact that blacks, more often than whites, have been the victims both of violence and of law and order efforts. This also gives context to the finding that blacks are less trusting than whites and less satisfied with the quality of their lives. The strong role of religion in southern black culture and the strength of southern black family structures have frequently been observed and both are apparent in the data, which show blacks more religiously committed than whites and more strongly opposed to abortion than whites.

Urbanism. The hypothesis that increased urbanism would foster value change in the South is supported by the data. White Southerners living in urban areas are somewhat more moderate on racial issues and definitely more tolerant than those living in rural areas; they are also more supportive of the goals of the feminist movement and less conservative on many moral questions. Those living in rural areas have stronger religious commitments and, it seems, a stronger commitment to gun ownership and hunting than those living in urban areas. Finally, those living in rural areas articulate a higher degree of satisfaction with their communities than do Southerners living in urban areas.

Income. Class divisions also are apparent in several issue areas. Low-income Southerners are more liberal on economic mat-

TABLE 1.3

Distinctions within the South

Item[a]	Race[b]	Urbanism[c]	Income[d]
RACE-1	.36	.14	.10
RACE-2	—	.13	.22
RACE-3	.30	-.01	.08
HLPMINR	.41	.11	-.09
BUSING		-.02	-.04
ATHTOL	.04	.20	.25
COMTOL	.02	.15	.23
HOMOTOL	.00	.16	.24
DEFSPDR	.10	.00	-.06
NATARMS	.02	.08	-.04
CONARMY	.05	.05	.09
RUSSIA	-.02	.05	.09
COMMUN	.15	.07	.03
PETRUST	-.21	.00	.17
PREMARSX	.16	.21	.11
HOMOSEX	-.07	.18	.04
SEXEDUC	.02	.08	.21
GRASS	.01	.13	.05
YOUNGEN	.00	.11	.16
XMARSEX	.09	.16	.05
TEENPILL	.00	.07	.22
PILL	-.10	.04	.14
PORNLAW	.14	.08	.05
DIVLAW	.20	.14	.02
FEM-1	.01	.13	.18
FEM-2	.09	.09	.28
ABORTSUM	-.17	.09	.13
PRAYER	-.10	.05	.05
ATTEND	-.12	.09	-.06
RELITEN	-.09	.07	.07
CONCLERG	-.04	.01	.04
GUNLAW	.07	.08	-.05
HUNT	.08	.22	-.20
HITOK	.15	-.04	-.14
SATCITY	.06	.09	-.06
SATJOB	.11	.00	-.04
HAPPY	.17	.04	-.09
SATFIN	.09	.06	-.17
NATSUM	.24	.02	-.03
EQWLTH	.24	-.06	-.20
CONFINAN	.05	.06	.03
CONBUS	.10	-.04	-.11
CONPUB	.00	.01	-.04
CUTSPDR	.22	-.06	-.12
CAPPUN	-.24	.03	.08
COURTS	-.15	-.03	.05

[a] See Table 1.1 for descriptions of the items and the southern response.
[b] Minus sign means blacks are more "southern" on the issue.
[c] Minus sign means urbanites are more "southern" on the issue.
[d] Minus sign means high-income respondents are more "southern" on the issue.

Note: Entries are betas indicating the explanatory power of each demographic variable with the effects of the other two controlled.

Source: Compiled by the author from National Opinion Research Center.

ters; they also are less trustful of others, more opposed to abortion, and stronger in their religious commitment than those of higher socioeconomic status. Those at the upper end of the socioeconomic scale are more moderate on racial matters, much more tolerant, more favorably disposed toward feminism, more liberal on several moral questions, and of course, more satisfied with their lives. They are also somewhat less supportive of the armed forces, less hostile to the Soviet Union, and more committed to the southern culture of violence than are the less well-off.[34]

CONCLUSION

Several conclusions can be drawn from the data, many of which will be obvious to those who have studied the South more persistently than I have. First, the South continues to be distinct. On almost every issue included in this analysis there was some overall difference between southern and northern respondents, and the difference was in the direction that would have been predicted based on various expectations about the South. Thus the South is, compared with the rest of the nation, more racist, less tolerant, more supportive of the military, less trusting, more puritanical, more sexist, more religious, more violent, more pleasing to live in, and more conservative on economic issues. The only findings contrary to expectations were that Southerners have more rather than less confidence in the federal government than the rest of the nation, and that when demographic variables are controlled, the southern attitude toward capital punishment and the treatment accorded to criminals by the courts is no different from that of the rest of the nation.

Second, the data also indicate that the magnitude of the distinctions between the South and the rest of the nation varies significantly across issue areas and that in no case does region explain an extraordinarily large percentage of the nationwide variance on an issue. Thus the highest beta in Table 1.1 is .24 for the second scale of racial issues, which means that even on this most regionally divisive set of items, region explains less than 6 percent of the variance in the nationwide sample. On the other current issues, regional divisions range from modest to minuscule. On defense spending and on some religious and moral issues there is a clear distinction between the South and the rest of the nation. However, on moral issues such as pornography and divorce, and on confidence in the clergy there are very narrow regional differences; on economic issues and the role of government the regional differences are virtually nil. Distinctions of the magnitude found here are, it would seem, a dubious basis for classifying the South as a distinct subculture.

Another set of conclusions underlines the diversity of southern opinions. While the South in the aggregate may not be very different from the rest of the country on most issues, the distinctiveness of certain Southerners is more persistent than others, and more important, Southerners differ significantly from each other. As many scholars have recognized, one must speak of an increasingly divided South with different patterns of divisions on different issues.

The traditional South does survive, but primarily among whites of relatively low economic status, especially those living in rural areas. This segment of the southern population is most distinct in its views from people of similar demographic characteristics living in other parts of the country. This group continues to be the most resistant to the advances of blacks, the most intolerant of deviant groups, and the most conservative on religious and other moral issues and on women's rights. However, it also displays some tendency toward economic liberalism and some dissatisfaction with the quality of life.

The mind of the new South is dominated by the more affluent white urban and suburban sectors who, while very conservative on economic and law and order issues, are also much more tolerant of deviant groups, less narrow in their views on moral questions, and more supportive of the women's movement. In addition, this group articulates a high degree of satisfaction with living and working environments.

Lying somewhere between the traditional South and the new South, apart from yet a part of each, is the black South. Black roots in the old South are manifest in the strength of black religious commitment and traditional family values, as demonstrated in the data by strong black opposition to abortion, significant opposition to birth control, and lack of tolerance for homosexuals. A residue of the old South is also seen in the strong opposition of southern blacks to violence and in the low levels of interpersonal trust that characterize this group. However, southern blacks constitute the most liberal part of the South on economic questions and on law and order issues, the most dissatisfied with the quality of southern life, and of course, the most concerned with elimination of racial inequalities.

One of the most striking conclusions from this analysis of divisions within the South is how little it challenges what social scientists know about the attitudes of the American people in general. The salutary effects of high socioeconomic status and urban living on racial, political, social, and sexual tolerance have been well documented. The economic conservatism and self-satisfaction of upper-status groups and the economic liberalism and discontent of those at the other end of the socioeconomic scale are hardly surprising. Similarly, a stronger religious commitment among the rural poor is a nearly global finding. Thus basic rules of political behavior seem to fit the

South as well as they fit the rest of the nation, which suggests that although the mind of the South may be somewhat distinctive from that of the rest of the nation, it functions and responds to environmental factors in much the same way as the mind of the non–South.

NOTES

1. See Laurence W. Moreland, Tod A. Baker, and Robert P. Steed, eds., Contemporary Southern Political Attitudes and Behavior (New York: Praeger, 1982); Jack Bass and Walter DeVries, The Transformation of Southern Politics (New York: Basic Books, 1976); William C. Havard, ed., The Changing Politics of the South (Baton Rouge: Louisiana State University Press, 1972); and Numan V. Bartley and Hugh D. Graham, Southern Politics and the Second Reconstruction (Baltimore: Johns Hopkins University Press, 1975).

2. The connection between sociocultural attitudes and political attitudes is discussed at great length in Michael L. Mezey, "Political Distrust: A Sociocultural Analysis" (Paper delivered at the Annual Meeting of the Midwest Political Science Association, Milwaukee, Wis., May 1982).

3. John Shelton Reed, The Enduring South: Subcultural Persistence in Mass Society (Lexington, Mass.: D. C. Heath, Lexington Books, 1972); and Norval D. Glenn, "Massification versus Differentiation: Some Trend Data from National Surveys," Social Forces 46 (December 1967): 172-80.

4. Ted Jelen, "Sources of Political Intolerance: The Case of the American South," in Contemporary Southern Political Attitudes and Behavior, ed. Laurence W. Moreland, Tod A. Baker, and Robert P. Steed (New York: Praeger, 1982), pp. 73-91.

5. Earl W. Hawkey, "Southern Conservatism, 1956-1976," in Contemporary Southern Political Attitudes and Behavior, ed. Moreland, Baker, and Steed, pp. 48-72.

6. Robert S. Erikson and Norman R. Luttbeg, American Public Opinion (New York: John Wiley & Sons, 1973), pp. 174-75, 200-1.

7. Bass and DeVries, The Transformation of Southern Politics, pp. 15-19.

8. See John C. McKinney and Linda Bourque, "The Changing South: National Incorporation of a Region," American Sociological Review 36 (June 1971): 399-412; and William C. Havard, "The South: A Shifting Perspective," in The Changing Politics of the South, ed. William C. Havard (Baton Rouge: Louisiana State University Press, 1972), p. 10.

9. Havard, "The South: A Shifting Perspective," pp. 4-5.

10. Reed, The Enduring South, p. 27; see also Hawkey, "Southern Conservatism, 1956-1976."

11. Joseph H. Fichter and George L. Maddox, "Religion in the South, Old and New," in The South in Continuity and Change, ed. John C. McKinney and Edgar T. Thompson (Durham, N.C.: Duke University Press, 1965), p. 361.

12. W. J. Cash, The Mind of the South (New York: Knopf, 1941), p. 335. See also Samuel S. Hill, Jr., ed., Religion and the Solid South (Nashville, Tenn.: Abingdon Press, 1972); and Thomas Daniel Young, "Religion, the Bible Belt, and the Modern South," in The American South, ed. Louis D. Rubin, Jr. (Baton Rouge: Louisiana State University Press, 1980), pp. 110-17.

13. See Franklin Frazier, The Negro Church in America (New York: Schocken Books, 1963); see also J. Milton Yinger, The Scientific Study of Religion (New York: Macmillan, 1970), chap. 15.

14. Reed, The Enduring South, pp. 84-85.

15. See Anne Firor Scott, The Southern Lady from Pedestal to Politics: 1830-1930 (Chicago: University of Chicago Press, 1970).

16. See Reed, The Enduring South, pp. 84-85. See also Cash, The Mind of the South, pp. 115-17.

17. Hawkey, "Southern Conservatism, 1956-1976," p. 64.

18. Cash, The Mind of the South, pp. 45-53.

19. Ibid., p. 31; see also Robert E. Botsch, "A Microanalytic Return to the Mind of the South," in Contemporary Southern Political Attitudes and Behavior, ed. Moreland, Baker, and Steed, pp. 24-47.

20. V. O. Key, Jr., Public Opinion and American Democracy (New York: Alfred A. Knopf, 1967), p. 102.

21. Havard, "The South: A Shifting Perspective," p. 6.

22. See ibid. See also Alfred O. Hero, Jr., The Southerner and World Affairs (Baton Rouge: Louisiana State University Press, 1965), chap. 3; and Tod A. Baker, Robert P. Steed, and Laurence W. Moreland, "Southern Distinctiveness and the Emergence of Party Competition: The Case of a Deep South State," in Contemporary Southern Political Attitudes and Behavior, ed. Moreland, Baker, and Steed, pp. 199-203.

23. Cash, The Mind of the South, p. 328.

24. Hawkey, "Southern Conservatism, 1956-1976," pp. 61-62.

25. Reed, The Enduring South, chap. 5. See also Botsch, "A Microanalytic Return," pp. 37-41; and Sheldon Hackney, "Southern Violence," in The History of Violence in America, ed. Hugh D. Graham and Ted R. Gurr (New York: Praeger, 1969), pp. 505-27.

26. Bass and DeVries, The Transformation of Southern Politics, pp. 7-8.

27. Jelen, "Sources of Political Intolerance."

28. On the importance and potential political significance of quality of life measures, see Angus Campbell, The Sense of Well-Being in America (New York: McGraw-Hill, 1981); and Angus Campbell, Philip E. Converse, and W. L. Rodgers, The Quality of American Life (New York: Russell Sage Foundation, 1976). See also Mezey, "Political Distrust."

29. For the full text of all items used in this analysis, see National Opinion Research Center, General Social Surveys, 1972-1980: Cumulative Codebook (Chicago: University of Chicago Press, July 1980). In order to protect the anonymity of respondents in certain small states, the National Opinion Research Center (NORC) identifies respondents by region and thus specific states cannot be retrieved. Because NORC uses the regional classification system developed by the Bureau of the Census, we must include respondents from Delaware, Maryland, West Virginia, Kentucky, Tennessee, and Oklahoma with respondents from the ten states that usually define the South (Virginia, North Carolina, South Carolina, Georgia, Florida, Mississippi, Alabama, Louisiana, Arkansas, and Texas). On occasion, different scales are used for the same issue area because the same questions are not always included on every survey. Therefore, scales were constructed for related items that appeared on the same survey or group of surveys.

30. The analysis of variance calculations were performed by the ANOVA program of the Statistical Package for the Social Sciences. See Norman H. Nie, C. Hadlai Hull, Jean G. Jenkins, Karin Steinbrenner, and Dale H. Bent, Statistical Package for the Social Sciences, 2d ed. (New York: McGraw-Hill, 1975), chap. 22. The eta and beta statistics were produced through ANOVA's multiple classification analysis option. The urban classification consists of respondents from the central cities and suburbs of the 112 largest standard metropolitan statistical areas. All others are classified as rural. Income is divided into three categories based on total family income. Under $10,000 is classified as low income; between $10,0,00 and $19,999 is classified as medium income; $20,000 and above is classified as high income. In instances where figures for family income were unavailable, respondents with less than a high school education were classified as low income, those with a high school degree were classified as medium income, and those with some college experience were classified as high income.

31. Items included in RACE-2 and RACE-3 were not asked of nonwhite respondents.

32. See Jelen, "Sources of Political Intolerance," p. 85.

33. See Christopher Lasch, "The Trouble with Black Power," in Old Memories, New Moods, ed. Peter I. Rose (New York: Atherton Press, 1970), pp. 267-91.

34. On the correlation between upper-income status and gun ownership, see James D. Wright and Linda L. Marston, "The Ownership of the Means of Destruction: Weapons in the United States," Social Problems 23 (October 1975): 93-107.

2

BORN-AGAIN POLITICS:
THE POLITICAL BEHAVIOR
OF EVANGELICAL
CHRISTIANS IN THE
SOUTH AND NON-SOUTH

Corwin Smidt

INTRODUCTION

The relationship between Americans' religious faith and practice and variations in their political attitudes and behavior has been,
and continues to be, elusive in nature. [1] Several factors suggest that
religion may play a significant role within American politics. Conventional wisdom assumes that a positive relationship exists between religiosity and political conservatism in attitudes and behavior. Moreover, public opinion polls have revealed that the religious beliefs and
practices of the American people are truly unique among Western political societies. [2] Finally, research has demonstrated that the effect
of religion can be, at times, quite powerful politically. [3]

Yet despite such assumptions and findings, political scientists
have tended to ignore the role of religion in American politics. Several factors appear to account for this general disinterest. First, it
has been usually assumed that religion constitutes a secondary,
rather than a primary, variable; essentially, it has been thought that
the "effect" of religion could be satisfactorily accounted for by variation in socioeconomic status among individuals—whether it be across
different religious groups, denominations, or levels of religious involvement. Second, it has been generally assumed that any remaining variance attributable to religious variables represents some dy-
ing vestige of influence from the past. Generally speaking, it has
been assumed that as scientific knowledge advanced, the process of
secularization would continue to diminish the scope and influence of
the religious sphere of life. [4] Finally, many studies have suggested
that the effect of religion upon political attitudes and behavior is relatively weak or nonexistent. For example, Robert Wuthnow in his
review of research conducted during the 1960s found that a majority

of the relationships reported indicated that religious conservatism in terms of commitment and/or belief was either unrelated, or negatively related, to political conservatism.[5]

However, two recent trends within American society have sparked renewed interest in the role of religion within American politics: (1) the apparent growth of political conservatism within the electorate and (2) the apparent growth and increased political militancy among Evangelical Christians. These parallel changes have prompted not only increased attention to the influence of religion upon electoral behavior, in general, but a new focus upon the political nature and electoral importance of Evangelical Christians, in particular. As yet there has been very little empirical study on the political beliefs and behavior of contemporary Evangelical Christians. Therefore, this chapter attempts to partially fill the void by analyzing the political attitudes of Evangelical Christians—and southern Evangelical Christians, in particular—and their electoral behavior in the 1980 presidential election.

EVANGELICALISM

Historical Background

Around 1940 various Christian leaders in this country adopted the label Evangelical in order to differentiate themselves from the two major divisions within Protestantism at the time, namely, Fundamentalism and Liberalism. These Evangelicals shared the concern of Fundamentalists for defending the faith against Liberalism's tendency to regard the Bible as only metaphorically true and Jesus Christ as merely an ethical prophet. However, Evangelicals were critical of Fundamentalism on at least three points: they objected to the anti-intellectualism associated with Fundamentalism,[6] they rejected the total otherworldliness concern that tended to characterize Fundamentalism,[7] and they rejected the extreme ecclesiastical separation practiced by Fundamentalists.[8]

Today these distinctions are still important, but perhaps—as was also true in the past—much more so among clerics than among parishioners. While Evangelicals continue to espouse many of the same doctrinal beliefs as Fundamentalists, they still tend to differ in attitudes toward cooperation with other Christians and toward the Christian's relationship to contemporary culture. Evangelicals tend to perceive themselves as disengaging orthodox Christianity from the excesses of Fundamentalism, while Fundamentalists tend to perceive Evangelicals as compromising with truth in order to achieve consensus. Thus for the most part Evangelicals do not like to be called Fundamentalists, and Fundamentalists do not like to be called Evangelicals.[9]

Definition

Any attempt to define the term Evangelical is fraught with difficulty. Analyses of historical and theological uses of the term have demonstrated just how difficult such a task really is. [10] Both the meaning of the term and the theological beliefs associated with Evangelicalism have changed over time.

Moreover, there is a complex variety of religious groups that either call themselves Evangelicals or that have been labeled as Evangelicals. For example, Robert Webber has identified 14 different religious subcultural groups within Evangelicalism, each expressing different types of emphases. [11] In addition, some theological polarization between younger and older Evangelicals[12] as well as between progressive and militant groups of Evangelicals may have taken place over the past two decades within each of these distinct subcultural groups. [13]

Thus, as James Guth has recognized, both strict and loose definitions of the term Evangelical have some undesirable consequences. [14] Strict definitions run the risk of excluding members of many religious groups traditionally known as Evangelicals. For example, many religious bodies, some dating back to the Reformation, have historically been known as Evangelical denominations (for example, the Evangelical United Brethren or the Evangelical Free Church). Yet members of such groups may not be identified as Evangelicals if strict definitions are employed. On the other hand, loose definitions of the term may include many believers (for example, Fundamentalists or "Charismatics") who might emphatically reject the Evangelical label.

However, in recent years there appears to be some development among scholars to use the term in a specific manner within contemporary culture. Certain characteristics are generally cited as the defining qualities of contemporary Evangelicals. Broadly speaking, Evangelicals are defined as those Christians who emphasize a personal relationship of the believer to Jesus Christ and who regard the Bible as being literally, rather than metaphorically, true. [15] But more narrowly, Evangelicals are specifically defined as having (1) a distinct type of personal relationship to Jesus Christ, that is, one in which the individual has had a spiritual encounter, whether gradual or instantaneous, known as a born-again experience, (2) a distinct literal view of scripture, that is, a strict literal view (inerrancy), rather than a loose literal view (infallibility), and (3) a distinct concern for encouraging others to believe in Jesus Christ. [16]

EVANGELICALISM IN THE SOUTH

Several factors suggest that a specific analysis of southern Evangelicals' political opinions and behavior would be particularly appropriate. First, almost every person studying southern life "has, sooner or later, recorded impressions about the pervasiveness and peculiarity of religious behavior and institutions in the region."[17] While religious patterns in the South still reveal a cultural distinctiveness, no such identifiable pattern exists in the North.[18]

Second, Evangelicals have been characterized as born-again Christians. And various scholars have noted that one hallmark of southern religious life has been both the demand for and the ability of individuals to state the "time when and place where" such a new birth began.[19] It is not too surprising, therefore, that nearly twice as many Southerners as non-Southerners were willing to state in 1980 that they have had a born-again experience.[20]

Third, it has been argued that historically speaking, there has been a close relationship between religion and politics in the South. Some scholars have contended, for example, that the "political solidarity of the South was conceived in an atmosphere of religious tension" in that denominational splits over theological beliefs occurred along geographical lines before the Civil War and that these schisms helped to prepare a foundation for southern political solidarity prior to the advent of the war.[21] In addition, other scholars have argued that at least until the relatively recent past, religion has been used "to maintain and retain the Old South."[22]

Finally, a specific analysis of electoral behavior of southern Evangelicals in the 1980 presidential election may be of particular interest given the unique nature of the presidential race of that year. Not only were all three major presidential candidates born-again Christians, but one candidate was a native son of the South. An analysis comparing and contrasting the electoral behavior of southern versus nonsouthern Evangelicals in this election permits one not only to analyze how cohesively Evangelicals may vote as a political bloc when confronted with a choice among coreligionists, but also to ascertain whether region may specify certain aspects of the relationship between religion and politics in the United States. Certainly the 1980 presidential election provides a good context in which to determine whether the political attitudes and behavior of Evangelicals are relatively similar nationally or whether their attitudes and behavior may be distinctively different within different political contexts.

METHODOLOGY

Data Base

The data to be analyzed are drawn from the 1980 presidential election study conducted by the Center for Political Studies (CPS) at the University of Michigan. This study contains a variety of questions pertaining to the religious faith and practices of the respondents as well as a host of questions relating to their political attitudes and behavior. More important, however, the study contains several new questions that permit, for the first time, direct identification of those respondents who are Evangelical Christians.

Operational Definitions

Three criteria were employed to differentiate Evangelical respondents from other respondents. First, respondents had to state that religion played an important part in their life. Second, respondents had to acknowledge that they viewed the Bible as "God's work and all it says is true." Finally, respondents had to report that they had had a born-again experience. Only those respondents meeting all three criteria were classified as Evangelicals.

Because previous questions developed by the Gallup organization to tap Evangelicals were not used in the Michigan study, this operational measure of Evangelicals differs somewhat from the operational measures initially employed by the Gallup Poll.[23] Nevertheless, as can be seen from Table 2.1, the distribution of Evangelicals resulting from the operational definition used in this chapter literally mirrors the distribution of Evangelicals found by Gallup during the same general cross section in time. Not only was the national distribution of Evangelicals equivalent across the two studies (19 percent), but the distributions of Evangelicals found within categories of sex, race, denomination, and age were virtually identical for both surveys as well.

The South is defined in this chapter according to the CPS Solid South regional classification, that is, those states of the former Confederacy minus Tennessee. Because the CPS sampling procedure is not representative at the state level, creation of a regional definition other than that employed by the CPS survey would violate the sampling design. Consequently, the CPS regional definition was utilized in order to maintain the representativeness of the specific subsample.[24]

TABLE 2.1

Distribution of Evangelicals Comparing Gallup Study with
Present Study
(in percent)

	Gallup Study[a]	Present Study[b]
National	19	19
Sex		
Male	15	15
Female	22	22
Race		
White	16	17
Other	36	34
Denomination		
Protestant	28	28
Catholic	6	5
Age		
18–24	13	15
25–29	15	17
30–49	19	20
50+	22	22

[a]Source: George Gallup, Jr., ed., Public Opinion 1980 (Wilmington, Del.: Scholarly Sources, 1981), p. 189. Interviews conducted during August 1980.

[b]Source: Compiled by the author from Center for Political Studies data.

DATA ANALYSIS

Distribution in the South

Given the operational definitions described in the previous section, it is possible to determine the extent to which Evangelical Christians may be found within the South. Actually, it appears that Evangelical Christians represent only a minority of voters in the South. As shown in Table 2.2, Evangelicals constitute 30.5 percent of the southern electorate. Nevertheless, the proportion of Evangelical Christians is especially high in the South in that less than 15 percent of the electorate outside the South could be classified as Evangelicals in 1980. Thus the southern states are distinctively Evangelical in

TABLE 2.2

Distribution of Evangelicals by Region

| | Region | |
	South	Non-South
Non-Evangelical (in percent)	69.5	85.2
Evangelical (in percent)	30.5	14.8
Total percent	100.0	100.0
(N)	(380)	(1,028)

Source: Compiled by the author from Center for Political Studies data.

terms of religious composition: one is twice as likely to find Evangelical Christians within the South as to find such Christians outside the South.

Social Composition

As can be seen from Table 2.3, southern Evangelicals differ from southern non-Evangelicals in terms of their social composition. While slightly more than half of southern non-Evangelicals are females, nearly two-thirds of southern Evangelicals are women. While slightly more than 14 percent of southern non-Evangelicals are blacks, nearly twice as many southern Evangelicals are blacks (25 percent). Similarly, southern Evangelicals are more likely to be older than their non-Evangelical counterparts and as a group are less well educated than southern non-Evangelicals.

Southern Evangelicals also tend to be more ideologically polarized than southern non-Evangelicals. Not only are southern Evangelicals more likely to be self-classified conservatives than southern non-Evangelicals (30.3 percent versus 25.8 percent), but they are more likely to classify themselves as ideological liberals as well (12.1 percent versus 7.7 percent). While it is true that many more southern Evangelicals willingly classified themselves as conservatives than liberals, it is important to recognize that the "Evangelical Right" appears to represent only a segment of those who can be classified as Evangelicals. Even within the South, less than one-third of the Evangelical Christians classified themselves as conservatives.

TABLE 2.3

Social and Political Composition of Evangelicals and
Non-Evangelicals, by Region
(in percent)

Social or Political Category	South		Nonsouthern	
	Non-Evangelical	Evangelical	Non-Evangelical	Evangelical
Sex				
Male	48.9	34.5	45.1	33.6
Female	51.1	65.5	54.9	66.4
Total	100.0	100.0	100.0	100.0
(N)	(264)	(116)	(876)	(152)
Race				
White	85.6	75.0	90.5	78.1
Black	14.4	25.0	9.5	21.9
Total	100.0	100.0	100.0	100.0
(N)	(264)	(116)	(874)	(151)
Age				
18–34	42.0	31.9	38.7	32.9
35–54	30.3	27.6	31.4	35.5
55 and over	27.7	40.5	30.0	31.6
Total	100.0	100.0	100.1	100.0
(N)	(264)	(116)	(874)	(152)
Education				
Not high school graduate	24.2	40.5	22.9	33.8
High school graduate	30.3	36.2	36.8	35.8
At least some college	45.5	23.3	40.3	30.5
Total	100.0	100.0	100.0	100.0
(N)	(264)	(116)	(874)	(151)
Ideology	25.8	30.3	19.6	35.2
Conservative	25.8	30.3	19.6	35.2
Moderate*	66.4	57.6	71.0	59.4
Liberal	7.7	12.1	9.5	5.5
Total	99.9	100.0	100.1	100.1
(N)	(182)	(66)	(620)	(91)
Party identification				
Democrat	44.5	54.4	36.6	43.4
Independent	35.9	33.4	38.1	24.0
Republican	19.6	12.3	25.3	32.7
Total	100.0	100.1	100.0	100.0
(N)	(254)	(114)	(858)	(150)

*Includes those respondents who classified themselves as only slightly
liberal or slightly conservative.

Source: Compiled by the author from Center for Political Studies data.

Finally, southern Evangelicals tend to be more Democratic and less Republican in partisan identification than southern non-Evangelicals. Not only is the proportion of Democratic partisan identifiers greater among southern Evangelicals than among southern non-Evangelicals, but the percentage of Republicans found among southern Evangelicals is less than that found among southern non-Evangelicals.

Similarly, southern Evangelicals also differ in social composition from their Evangelical brothers and sisters outside the South. Other than with regard to gender and race, southern Evangelicals tend to be different from nonsouthern Evangelicals in terms of almost every social characteristic analyzed. For example, southern Evangelicals tend to have a slightly higher composition of blacks than do nonsouthern Evangelicals. Likewise, southern Evangelicals have a higher proportion of older and less well educated voters than do nonsouthern Evangelicals and a lower proportion of self-proclaimed conservatives and self-classified Republicans than do their coreligionists outside the South.

However, when one analyzes the social composition of white Evangelicals only, one finds the differences tend to change somewhat. The appropriate data are presented in Table 2.4. For example, while previously noted differences in terms of sex, age, and education among Evangelicals and non-Evangelicals within the South remain relatively unchanged, white Evangelicals in the South tend to be much more conservative in ideological orientation than southern white non-Evangelicals. Moreover, southern white Evangelicals are much more Democratic and less Republican in partisan identification than southern non-Evangelicals.

Similarly, many of the previously noted differences between southern and nonsouthern Evangelicals become even more pronounced when one analyzes white Evangelicals only. As can be seen from Table 2.4, age differences between southern and nonsouthern Evangelicals become enhanced when one examines white Evangelicals only. For example, while a plurality of southern white Evangelicals are 55 years of age or older (41.4 percent), a plurality of nonsouthern white Evangelicals are found within the 18-to-34 age bracket (36.4 percent). Similarly, differences between southern and nonsouthern Evangelicals in terms of partisan identification tend to become greater when one examines white respondents only. While a plurality of white southern Evangelicals classified themselves as Democrats (47.6 percent), a plurality of white nonsouthern Evangelicals classified themselves as Republicans (41.0 percent).

Only in one important respect do previously noted differences between southern and nonsouthern Evangelicals disappear when whites are examined only—and that is in terms of ideological orientations. When blacks are removed from the analysis, the ideological orienta-

TABLE 2.4

Social and Political Composition of White Evangelicals and
Non-Evangelicals by Region
(in percent)

Social or Political Category	South Non-Evangelical	South Evangelical	Non-South Non-Evangelical	Non-South Evangelical
Sex				
Male	49.6	34.5	44.9	33.1
Female	50.4	65.5	55.1	66.9
Total	100.0	100.0	100.0	100.0
(N)	(226)	(87)	(789)	(118)
Age				
18–34	41.2	33.3	38.0	36.4
35–54	30.1	25.3	31.2	33.9
55 and over	28.8	41.4	30.8	29.7
Total	100.0	100.0	100.0	100.0
(N)	(226)	(87)	(789)	(118)
Education				
Not high school graduate	21.2	34.5	21.5	27.4
High school graduate	30.5	37.9	37.6	38.5
At least some college	48.2	27.6	40.8	34.2
Total	99.9	100.0	99.9	100.1
(N)	(226)	(87)	(789)	(117)
Ideology				
Conservative	26.4	37.1	20.3	38.8
Moderate*	68.6	59.3	70.4	58.8
Liberal	4.9	3.7	9.3	2.5
Total	99.9	100.1	100.0	100.1
(N)	(163)	(54)	(577)	(80)
Party identification				
Democrat	40.4	47.7	33.6	31.6
Independent	37.2	37.2	38.9	27.4
Republican	22.5	15.1	27.4	41.0
Total	100.1	99.9	99.9	100.0
(N)	(218)	(86)	(776)	(117)

*Includes those respondents who classified themselves as only slightly liberal or slightly conservative.

Source: Compiled by the author from Center for Political Studies data.

tions found among southern and nonsouthern Evangelicals are virtually identical. Not only are southern and nonsouthern whites much more likely to classify themselves as conservatives than as liberals, but the proportion of conservatives found among southern white Evangelicals (37.1 percent) mirrors the proportion found among nonsouthern white Evangelicals (38.8 percent). Yet even among white Evangelicals only, just a little more than one-third of such religionists willingly place themselves on the right of the political spectrum.

Issue Orientations

Tables 2.5 and 2.6 compare and contrast the issue stands of southern white Evangelicals and non-Evangelicals with those of nonsouthern white Evangelicals and non-Evangelicals in terms of their respective orientations toward economic and social issues. Several considerations prompted a decision to restrict subsequent analysis to white respondents only. Not only do blacks tend to exhibit different political attitudes and behavior than whites, but blacks are also more likely to be found among Evangelicals than among non-Evangelicals. Thus, even though blacks constitute a minority within the ranks of Evangelicals, the influence of racial differences in attitudes and behavior would be greater among Evangelicals than among non-Evangelicals. Therefore, to control for such racial differences, subsequent analysis will be restricted to white respondents only.

As can be seen from Table 2.5, southern Evangelicals tend to be more liberal on the average in their economic issue orientations than are southern non-Evangelicals. On three of the four economic issues analyzed, the mean scores of southern Evangelicals on a seven-point scale are more liberal than those found among southern non-Evangelicals. Southern Evangelicals, as a whole, are more likely than southern non-Evangelicals to favor maintaining government services, reducing unemployment instead of inflation, and guaranteeing jobs by the government. Only with respect to governmental aid to minorities are southern white Evangelicals on the average less liberal than their non-Evangelical counterparts in the area of economic matters.

On the other hand, white Evangelicals outside the South tend, as a whole, to be more conservative in economic issue orientations than non-Evangelicals outside the South. Only with regard to reducing unemployment are nonsouthern Evangelicals as a whole more liberal than non-Evangelicals outside the South. However, there is little difference in the mean scores between Evangelicals and non-Evangelicals outside the South on the issue of reducing governmental services; and Evangelicals outside the South are definitely more conservative than

TABLE 2.5

Economic Issue Orientations among White Evangelicals and Non-Evangelicals by Region

Issue Scale	South				Non–South			
	Non–Evangelical	(N)	Evangelical	(N)	Non–Evangelical	(N)	Evangelical	(N)
Reduce government services	4.02	(188)	3.92	(72)	3.77	(657)	3.78	(97)
Reduce inflation rather than employment	4.09	(137)	4.02	(46)	4.05	(476)	3.59	(64)
Government aid to minorities	4.87	(198)	5.01	(70)	4.60	(689)	4.89	(97)
Government guarantee of jobs	4.54	(196)	4.26	(70)	4.56	(662)	4.87	(98)

Note: Decimal figures are mean scores on the indicated issue scale. A higher score indicates a more conservative orientation.

Source: Compiled by the author from Center for Political Studies data.

non-Evangelicals outside the South in terms of their positions on governmental aid to minorities and governmental ensurance of jobs for everyone.

Yet, despite their relative conservatism, Evangelicals outside the South tend to be more economically liberal than their Evangelical brothers and sisters within the South. In fact, the difference in mean scores between southern and nonsouthern Evangelicals tends to be as great, if not greater, than the difference in mean scores between Evangelicals and non-Evangelicals outside the South.

With regard to social issues, however, a somewhat different pattern prevails. First, regardless of whether one discusses the role of women in society, the desirability of busing to achieve integration, the place of prayer in public schools, or the right to have an abortion, Evangelicals as a whole tend to be more conservative than non-Evangelicals. On such social issues the impact of region does not appear to have as great an influence as the impact of religion. While the mean scores for southern Evangelicals tend to be slightly more conservative in nature than the mean scores for Evangelicals outside the South, the mean scores of Evangelicals, regardless of region, are decidedly more conservative in direction than the mean scores for non-Evangelicals.

In terms of issue orientations, therefore, it seems necessary to differentiate between the economic and social issue orientations found among Evangelicals. On economic issues Evangelicals tend to be divided within their own ranks. On such issues there tends to be greater similarity along regional lines than along religious lines. On social issues, however, Evangelicals appear to be united, and regional differences in attitudes among Evangelicals are much less apparent.

This lack of consensus among Evangelicals on economic and political issues has prompted Seymour Lipset and Earl Raab to conclude that "the term 'evangelical' is rather meaningless when interpreting reaction to general political issues."[25] But such a finding should not be too surprising. Relationships between religious and political beliefs are most likely to be demonstrated when the political implications associated with particular religious beliefs are fairly direct.[26] Political issues that tend to be structured and perceived as involving moral questions are much more likely to be affected by specific religious beliefs than are political issues that tend not to be so structured and/or perceived. The lack of consensus among Evangelicals on economic issues and the greater unity among Evangelicals on certain social issues are in keeping with such expectations.

TABLE 2.6

Social Issue Orientations among White Evangelicals and Non-Evangelicals by Region

Issue Scale	South				Non-South			
	Non-Evangelical	(N)	Evangelical	(N)	Non-Evangelical	(N)	Evangelical	(N)
Role of women	2.75	(216)	3.70	(80)	2.74	(738)	3.74	(111)
Bus to integrate	6.28	(216)	6.60	(81)	6.25	(736)	6.37	(111)
Prayer in public schools	4.13	(171)	4.90	(80)	3.60	(622)	4.58	(106)
Abortion	2.21	(217)	2.98	(85)	2.22	(770)	2.84	(114)

Note: Decimal figures are mean scores on the indicated issue scale. A higher score indicates a more conservative orientation.

Source: Compiled by the author from Center for Political Studies data.

Politicization

A great deal of attention has been given to the fact that Evangelical groups worked hard at increasing voter turnout within their ranks during the 1980 presidential election. Organizations such as the Moral Majority sought to enlist their members to establish registration drives within their congregations. Apparently, such efforts were motivated in part by polling data suggesting that 30 percent of all nonvoters actually attended church services three times a week and that a much smaller percentage of Evangelicals were registered to vote than non-Evangelicals.[27]

Was there an influx of large numbers of newly registered, Evangelical Christians during the 1980 election? Of all the regions, voting turnout increased only in the South. And some have argued that the Evangelical and Fundamentalist New Right groups were largely responsible for this particular increase.[28]

Table 2.7 analyzes the level of politicization found among white Evangelicals and non-Evangelicals according to the regions of the country in which they live. Generally speaking, the data tend to substantiate the following contentions: (1) that in the past Evangelicals were less likely to vote in presidential elections than non-Evangelicals, (2) that regardless of region Evangelicals were as politicized as non-Evangelicals in the 1980 election, and (3) that the apparent increase in politicization among Evangelicals was most evident within the southern states.

As Table 2.7 shows, a much larger proportion of southern non-Evangelicals than Evangelicals reported they had voted in all or most of the presidential elections prior to 1980 (70.5 percent versus 61.1 percent, respectively). Moreover, this apparent historic difference in voting turnout rate shown by southern Evangelicals and non-Evangelicals does not appear to be unique to the South. Nonsouthern Evangelicals and non-Evangelicals indicated they tended to turn out to vote in presidential elections in much the same pattern as that reported by their counterparts within the South. Perhaps, given the lower educational levels found among Evangelicals, such differences might be expected. But whatever the contributing factors involved, it would appear that Evangelicals both in and out of the South have, in the past, been underrepresented at the polls.

However, the lower turnout rate generally found among white Evangelicals appears to have changed dramatically in the 1980 presidential election. Outside the South, the proportion of Evangelicals who reported they had voted (74.6 percent) slightly exceeds that reported by non-Evangelicals (73.3 percent). Even more dramatic, however, is the difference in reported turnout between Evangelicals and non-Evangelicals within the South. While only 65.9 percent of

TABLE 2.7

Politicization of White Evangelicals and Non-Evangelicals by Region
(in percent)

	South		Non-South	
	Non-Evangelical	Evangelical	Non-Evangelical	Evangelical
Voting turnout in prior presidential elections				
All/most	70.5	61.1	73.2	60.8
Some/none	29.5	38.9	26.8	39.2
Total	100.0	100.0	100.0	100.0
(N)	(190)	(72)	(744)	(115)
Voted in 1980				
Yes	65.9	77.0	73.3	74.6
No	34.1	23.0	26.7	25.4
Total	100.0	100.0	100.0	100.0
(N)	(226)	(87)	(791)	(118)
Tried to influence others in 1980				
Yes	30.0	35.1	30.0	29.9
No	70.0	64.9	70.0	70.1
Total	100.0	100.0	100.0	100.0
(N)	(207)	(77)	(789)	(117)

Source: Compiled by the author from Center for Political Studies data.

non-Evangelical whites in the South reported they had voted, 77.0 percent of the southern white Evangelicals did so. Thus, of the groups analyzed, southern white Evangelicals appear to have been the most evident at the polls on election day in 1980. This turnout rate among white southern Evangelicals is all the more remarkable if one recalls that such religionists in the South tend to be older women with a relatively low level of education—social traits generally associated with lower levels of turnout.

This general pattern of politicization reflected in reported turnout is also evident in terms of reported attempts to influence the votes of others in the last election. The proportion of non-Evangelicals, regardless of region, and the proportion of nonsouthern Evangelicals stating they had tried to persuade others were literally identical. Of the groups analyzed, only southern Evangelicals appear to have been distinct in terms of their efforts to persuade others how to vote in particular races in the last presidential election.

Were segments of the Evangelical community who previously were relatively apathetic mobilized politically in 1980? Table 2.8 attempts to answer this question by analyzing the level of voter turnout found among white Evangelicals and non-Evangelicals while controlling for region and prior levels of politicization. The respondent's pattern of turnout in previous presidential elections was used as an indicator of the respondent's level of politicization prior to the 1980 election.

It is evident from the data presented in Table 2.8 that Evangelicals, regardless of region and prior levels of politicization, turned out to vote in higher proportions than non-Evangelicals. But the data further suggest that many Evangelicals in the South who previously tended to be relatively uninvolved politically were, in fact, mobilized to vote in the 1980 election. More specifically, the data indicate that while 46.4 percent of southern white Evangelicals who were characterized by a low level of politicization prior to 1980 reported voting in the last election, the corresponding rate is only about one-third as great (16.1 percent) among non-Evangelicals.

Thus, contrary to arguments made elsewhere, the data analyzed here suggest that efforts to mobilize the Evangelical constituency for political purposes was rather successful, at least in terms of politicization.[29] This apparent success was particularly evident in the South, the major base of Evangelicalism. On the basis of the data presented in Tables 2.7 and 2.8, it appears that not only were those previously politicized segments of the Evangelical community highly politicized in 1980, but also a relatively large, politically apathetic segment of the southern Evangelical community was in fact mobilized in 1980 to vote.

TABLE 2.8

Voter Turnout among White Evangelicals and Non-Evangelicals in 1980, Controlling for Prior Politicization and Region

(in percent)

Voting Turnout in Prior Presidential Elections	South		Non-South	
	Non-Evangelical	Evangelical	Non-Evangelical	Evangelical
All/most				
Voted in 1980	90.3	93.2	88.2	98.6
Did not vote in 1980	9.7	6.8	11.8	1.4
Total	100.0	100.0	100.0	100.0
(N)	(134)	(44)	(544)	(70)
Some/none				
Voted in 1980	16.1	46.4	33.5	35.6
Did not vote in 1980	83.9	53.6	66.5	64.4
Total	100.0	100.0	100.0	100.0
(N)	(56)	(28)	(200)	(45)

Source: Compiled by the author from Center for Political Studies data.

44

Partisanship

While Evangelicals were, relatively speaking, highly politicized in the 1980 presidential election, it remains to be determined whether the mobilized Evangelicals contributed significantly to Republican success in the last election. The data shown in Table 2.9 present patterns in presidential voting among white Evangelicals and non-Evangelicals according to the region in which they live.

It is evident, first, from Table 2.9 that it was not the southern white Evangelicals who gave Carter his margin of victory against Ford in 1976. On the basis of recall four years later, it appears that southern white Evangelicals voted overwhelmingly for Ford in 1976 (59.2 percent), while white non-Evangelicals in the South gave Carter a slight edge in terms of their ballots during the same year (51.9 percent). Perhaps the appeal of a fellow Southerner tilted many white non-Evangelicals within the South to vote for Carter in 1976, but the candidacy of not only a Southerner but a born-again Southerner was not sufficient to attract the support of even a majority of Carter's coreligionists in the South during the 1976 presidential election.

On the other hand, outside the South it was the white Evangelicals who, despite their Republican tendencies, went overwhelmingly for Carter in 1976 (57.3 percent), while their non-Evangelical counterparts voted primarily for Ford (53.8 percent). Thus it appears that the professed religious faith of Carter was particularly appealing to white Evangelicals outside the South in 1976. And it may very well be that this overwhelming support for Carter among such highly Republican Evangelicals actually provided Carter with the margin of victory he needed in many of the key states outside the South.

However, in 1980 Evangelicals regardless of region voted overwhelmingly for Reagan. While 61.2 percent of white Evangelicals in the South voted for Reagan, 67.8 percent of their coreligionists outside the South did so. On the other hand, non-Evangelicals tended to vote less Republican in their presidential vote than did Evangelicals— with 59.0 percent and 54.7 percent of the white non-Evangelicals within and outside the South stating, respectively, that they had voted for Reagan.

But, of the groups analyzed, it is evident that the greatest amount of aggregate change in voting pattern between 1976 and 1980 occurs primarily among non-Evangelicals in the South and among Evangelicals outside the South. Reagan fared little better among Evangelicals in the South in 1980 than Ford had done in 1976, but Reagan captured over 10 percent more of the southern white non-Evangelical vote in 1980 than Ford had done in the previous presidential election. Outside the South, the proportion of white non-Evangelicals voting Republican changes little between 1976 and 1980, but the proportion

TABLE 2.9

Partisanship in Presidential Voting among White Evangelicals and Non-Evangelicals by Region
(in percent)

	South		Non-South	
	Non-Evangelical	Evangelical	Non-Evangelical	Evangelical
Reported vote in 1976				
Ford	48.1	59.2	53.8	42.7
Carter	51.9	40.8	46.2	57.3
Total	100.0	100.0	100.0	100.0
(N)	(135)	(49)	(520)	(75)
Reported vote in 1980				
Reagan	59.0	61.2	54.7	67.8
Carter	34.7	38.8	33.2	28.7
Anderson	6.3	0.0	12.1	3.4
Total	100.0	100.0	100.0	99.9
(N)	(144)	(62)	(545)	(87)
Pattern of reported vote, 1976–1980				
Ford–Reagan	46.4	55.8	48.3	41.2
Ford–Carter	6.4	4.7	6.5	2.9
Carter–Reagan	15.5	16.3	14.4	27.9
Carter–Carter	31.8	23.3	30.8	27.9
Total	100.1	100.1	100.0	99.9
(N)	(110)	(43)	(402)	(68)

Source: Compiled by the author from Center for Political Studies data.

of white Evangelicals voting Republican increases over 25 percent from the proportion found four years earlier.

These aggregate changes are also reflected in the pattern of swing voting presented in the bottom part of Table 2. 9. It is evident that the level of swing voting between 1976 and 1980 was much the same for southern Evangelicals and non-Evangelicals. For example, while 15. 5 percent of southern white non-Evangelicals reported having voted for Carter in 1976 and for Reagan in 1980, a slightly higher percentage did so among corresponding Evangelicals (16. 3 percent). Thus the rate of defection from Carter is hardly greater among southern white Evangelicals than it is among southern white non-Evangelicals.

Nevertheless, it is also evident that this pattern in swing voting found among southern voters is quite different from the pattern evident among voters outside the South. While white Evangelicals in the South did not abandon Carter at a higher rate than that found among southern non-Evangelicals, white Evangelicals outside the South jumped off the Carter bandwagon at a rate nearly double that found among non-Evangelicals outside the South (27. 9 percent versus 14. 4 percent, respectively). It is not totally clear whether those non-southern Evangelicals swinging to Reagan in 1980 were essentially returning home to the Republican fold in 1980 or simply voting for an alternative "Evangelical" candidate who happened to be Republican.[30] But whatever the case, Carter experienced his greatest loss of support among Evangelical voters outside the South.

Thus, as Fairbanks suggests, it may very well be that the Evangelical vote was much more significant in 1976 than it was in 1980.[31] In 1976 Evangelical Christians with Republican leanings forsook Ford and supported the candidacy of Carter—presumably because of his willingness to identify himself as a born-again Christian. But in 1980 it appears that being a born-again Christian was not sufficient to keep such Republican Evangelicals within the Carter camp.

It may be, however, that the impact of the Evangelical vote was a more significant factor in subpresidential elections than in the presidential election of 1980. In order to ascertain the partisanship of Evangelicals and non-Evangelicals in subpresidential voting, the reported votes of respondents for candidates for the House of Representatives and the Senate are analyzed. The data are presented in Table 2. 10.

As can be seen from Table 2. 10, southern white Evangelicals tend to vote slightly more Democratic than southern white non-Evangelicals in terms of congressional voting. While 59. 3 percent of the Evangelicals stated they voted for Democratic congressional candidates, 56. 3 percent of the non-Evangelicals so reported. However, the reverse is true with regard to voting for the U. S. Senate. While

58. 0 percent of the southern white non-Evangelicals stated they had voted for Republican candidates for the U.S. Senate, nearly two-thirds (65.5 percent) of the southern white Evangelicals did so. In fact, southern white Evangelicals, despite their greater Democratic loyalties, voted more Republican for senatorial candidates (65.5 percent) than did nonsouthern white Evangelicals (59.7 percent).

Given the differences in the relative distribution of partisan identification found among white Evangelicals and non-Evangelicals, it may be advantageous to control for the partisan identification of respondents while analyzing differences in the voting behavior between Evangelicals and non-Evangelicals. When such controls are introduced several distinct patterns emerge from the data, as can be seen from Table 2.11.

First, it appears that self-classified Democratic and Republican Evangelicals in the South tend to vote somewhat differently from self-classified Independent southern Evangelicals. Southern Evangelicals who classified themselves as Democrats tend to vote more Democratic, regardless of the office analyzed, than do Democratic non-Evangelicals in the South. The same pattern appears to be true among southern Evangelicals who classified themselves as Republicans—although the number of Republican Evangelicals in the South in 1980 was so small as to make the resulting percentages somewhat unstable. Nevertheless, the patterns are consistent among such southern Evangelical Republicans. White Evangelicals in the South who classified themselves as Republicans tend to vote more Democratic, regardless of the office analyzed, than do southern non-Evangelical Republicans.

Second, southern white Evangelicals who classified themselves as Independents are much more Republican in their voting behavior than are their non-Evangelical counterparts. While southern white non-Evangelical Independents tended to vote somewhat Republican in 1980, self-classified Independent Evangelicals voted overwhelmingly so. For example, while only 27.5 percent of southern non-Evangelical Independents voted for Carter in 1980, only 8.7 percent of the southern Evangelical Independents did so; while 67.6 percent of the non-Evangelical Independents in the South voted for the Democratic candidate for Congress, only 35.0 percent of the Evangelical Independents did so. Likewise, a much smaller percentage of Evangelical Independents reported having voted for Democratic candidates for the U.S. Senate (9.1 percent) than did non-Evangelical Independents in the South (35.3 percent).

Third, it is evident that nonsouthern Evangelicals are much more consistent in their voting patterns. Regardless of their partisan identification, nonsouthern white Evangelicals tended to vote more Republican in 1980 than did corresponding non-Evangelicals. Nonsouthern Evangelicals who classified themselves as Democrats are

TABLE 2.10

Partisanship in Voting for Congressmen and Senators among White Evangelicals and Non-Evangelicals
by Region
(in percent)

	South		Non-South	
	Non-Evangelical	Evangelical	Non-Evangelical	Evangelical
Vote for U.S. Representative				
Democrat	56.5	59.3	50.7	32.1
Republican	43.5	40.7	49.3	67.9
Total	100.0	100.0	100.0	100.0
(N)	(124)	(59)	(507)	(81)
Vote for U.S. Senator				
Democrat	42.0	34.5	54.5	40.3
Republican	58.0	65.5	45.5	59.7
Total	100.0	100.0	100.0	100.0
(N)	(69)	(29)	(387)	(62)

Source: Compiled by the author from Center for Political Studies data.

TABLE 2.11

Voting Behavior among White Evangelicals and Non-Evangelicals, Controlling for Partisan Identification and Region (in percent)

Partisan Identification	South		Nonsouthern	
	Non-Evangelical	Evangelical	Non-Evangelical	Evangelical
Democrat				
President	66.7	67.7	75.6	74.1
(N)	(57)	(31)	(168)	(27)
U.S. representative	68.0	81.5	76.9	59.3
(N)	(50)	(27)	(173)	(27)
U.S. senator	65.6	77.8	87.0	76.2
(N)	(32)	(9)	(138)	(21)
Independent				
President	27.5	8.7	30.9	18.8
(N)	(40)	(23)	(149)	(16)
U.S. representative	67.6	35.0	53.5	18.8
(N)	(37)	(20)	(172)	(16)
U.S. senator	35.3	9.1	58.8	38.5
(N)	(17)	(11)	(121)	(13)
Republican				
President	2.6	16.7	4.9	4.9
(N)	(38)	(12)	(162)	(41)
U.S. representative	29.7	50.0	20.0	18.4
(N)	(37)	(12)	(160)	(38)
U.S. senator	10.0	22.2	25.2	14.3
(N)	(20)	(9)	(127)	(28)

Note: Decimal figures represent the percentage having reported they voted Democratic.

Source: Compiled by the author from Center for Political Studies data.

50

more likely to vote Republican than non-Evangelical Democrats outside the South, and the same is true among nonsouthern Independents
and Republicans as well. Moreover, this pattern is evident whether
on analyzed presidential or subpresidential electoral behavior. Regardless of the partisan identifications of the respondents or the offices analyzed, nonsouthern Evangelicals vote more Republican than
do non-Evangelicals outside the South.

CONCLUSION

On the basis of the data analyzed in this chapter, several conclusions may be drawn about the nature and role of Evangelicals in
southern politics today. First, it is evident that only a minority of
southern white Evangelicals are, by nature, across-the-board political conservatives. Not only are less than 40 percent of southern white
Evangelicals willing to classify themselves as political conservatives,
but southern white Evangelicals are more likely to favor governmental intervention in the economy than are southern non-Evangelicals.
Only with regard to selected social issues does the conservatism of
Evangelicals become evident. Southern Evangelicals tend to be cultural conservatives, particularly when issues involve traditional moral
values.
Thus, while Evangelicals may have aligned with the secular Right
in supporting particular candidates in 1980, Evangelicals as a whole
are likely to find their relationship with the secular Right to be rather
frustrating. While secular conservatives appear to be primarily concerned with economic issues and secondarily with social issues,
Evangelicals are primarily concerned with certain social issues. As
secular conservatives focus on economic issues and ignore social issues, Evangelicals are likely to become somewhat impatient with such
conservatives, and new alignments and political strategies may become evident.
Second, it is evident that the political power of southern Evangelicals as a voting bloc can be easily overestimated. Evangelicals
are a politically important segment of the electorate—but any large
group is. Despite the greater public attention given to Evangelical
voters in 1980, they have not suddenly emerged as a totally new factor
in the country's political life. And given the considerable subcultural,
theological, and political diversity found among Evangelicals, it is
highly unlikely that any efforts to establish a unified political movement among Evangelicals as a whole will ultimately prove to be successful.
Third, it is evident that the political power of southern Evangelicals as a voting bloc can also be easily underestimated. Analyses

of electoral change must pay attention not only to partisan divisions within the electorate but to changes in its size and social composition as well. The processes of mobilization and demobilization that "pull people over the threshold of indifference to become voters, or alternatively, let them slide back, have important effects on electoral outcomes."[32] In the past Evangelicals have been, relatively speaking, uninvolved politically. If efforts to politically organize even a segment of the Evangelical community (as evident in 1980) continue to prove successful, the results could be politically significant. Any small shift in the composition of the electorate, whatever its nature, can easily change the relative balance of power in many key electoral states. And efforts to mobilize Evangelicals can easily influence state and local races as well—particularly in low-visibility primaries and caucuses, which normally tend to be characterized by relatively low voter turnout.

Fourth, it is evident that the proportion of behavioral Republicans found among southern white Evangelicals is substantially larger than the proportion of self-classified Republicans found among such religionists. Republican voting is particularly evident among southern white Evangelicals who classified themselves as Independents. Moreover, voting Republican among white Evangelical Independents is not limited to presidential voting alone, but is evident in congressional and senatorial voting as well. Such highly partisan voting behavior among southern Evangelical Independents may be an important step in the alignment of such Evangelicals within Republican ranks. Previous research has demonstrated that the process of adopting a partisan self-image among self-classified Independents is related to the partisan nature of the respondent's voting behavior. When self-classified Independents engage in highly partisan voting behavior, they are subsequently more likely to change their self-classification and adopt a partisan identification congruent with their partisan behavior than are those Independents who do not vote in a highly partisan manner. [33]

Finally, it is evident that researchers on the political attitudes and behavior of religious groups must exhibit greater sensitivity to various distinctions that may be salient among religiously conservative Christians. For example, Fundamentalists have been frequently defined in such a manner as to make the classification either highly detailed or meaningless. [34] It may, therefore, be advantageous to distinguish between Fundamentalists and Evangelicals—particularly when analyzing the political characteristics of religious groups in the South.

For many, Evangelicals and Fundamentalists may seem to be one and the same, and obviously differences between the two expressions of Orthodox Christianity are only relatively important. From the perspective of supernaturalism versus secularism, there is little difference between the theological positions of Fundamentalists and Evangelicals. But differences between Fundamentalists and Evangelicals do exist in terms of methodology and doctrine, and these differences have important political implications.[35] Given that the South is also considered to be the home of religious Fundamentalism in the United States, future attempts to distinguish between Evangelicals and Fundamentalists may enable scholars to more clearly specify the nature of the relationship between the religious and political spheres of life in the South today.

NOTES

1. In part, the continual nature of the problem is because both religion and political beliefs are multidimensional in nature. Each variable has a variety of conceptual or operational definitions.

2. John Benson, "The Polls: A Rebirth of Religion?" Public Opinion Quarterly 45 (Winter 1981): 576-85; and "Opinion Roundup," Public Opinion 2 (March-May 1979): 38-39.

3. See, for example, David Knoke, "Religion, Stratification and Politics: American in the 1960s," American Journal of Political Science 18 (May 1974): 331-45; David Knoke, "Religious Involvement and Political Behavior," Sociological Quarterly 15 (Winter 1974): 51-65; Kent Tedin, "Religious Preference and Pro/Anti Activism on the Equal Rights Amendment Issue," Pacific Sociological Review 21 (January 1978): 58-66; and Ronald Wimberley, "Civil Religion and the Choice for President: Nixon in '72," Social Forces 59 (September 1980): 44-61.

4. Literature on the secularization thesis is extensive. For a review of some of the present controversies on the topic, see Bryan Wilson, "Return of the Sacred," Journal of the Scientific Study of Religion 18 (September 1979): 268-80. Several different explanations have been advanced to account for the rise in Evangelical prominence over the past decade: a status thesis, a cultural defense thesis, and a "failure of modernity" thesis. See, for example, Seymour Martin Lipset and Earl Raab, "The Election and the Evangelicals," Commentary 71 (March 1981): 25-31; James Guth, "The Politics of the 'Evangelical Right'" (Paper presented at the 1981 Annual Meeting of the American Political Science Association, New York, September 3-6); and John Simpson, "Support for the Moral Majority and Status Politics in Contemporary America" (Paper presented at the 1981 Annual Meeting of the Association for the Sociology of Religion, Toronto, August 21-24).

5. Robert Wuthnow, "Religious Commitment and Conservatism: In Search of an Elusive Relationship," in Religion in Sociological Perspective, ed. Charles Glock (Belmont, Calif.: Wadsworth, 1973), pp. 117-32.

6. For example, rather than establishing Bible institutes, Evangelicals have generally created colleges and universities; rather than condemning higher criticism as a method of biblical analysis, they have tended to appreciate the techniques of higher criticism without necessarily accepting all of its previous conclusions; and rather than defending biblical inerrancy, Evangelicals are more likely to espouse biblical infallibility.

7. In part, this may be attributed to the fact that dispensational premillennialism is generally accepted within Fundamentalist circles, while much greater diversity is evident among Evangelicals in terms of their approach to eschatology. See, for example, William Wells, Welcome to the Family: An Introduction to Evangelical Christianity (Downers Grove, Ill.: Inter-Varsity Press, 1979), pp. 156-58.

8. For example, Fundamentalists have been critical of Billy Graham's willingness to work with liberal denominations in planning and promoting his Evangelistic campaigns. See Jerry Falwell, ed., The Fundamentalist Phenomenon (Garden City, N.Y.: Doubleday, 1981), pp. 146-51.

9. Richard Quebedeaux, The Young Evangelicals (New York: Harper & Row, 1974), p. 19.

10. See, for example, Robert Webber, Common Roots: A Call to Evangelical Maturity (Grand Rapids, Mich.: Zondervan, 1978), pp. 26-30; and Richard Mouw, "New Alignments," in Against the World for the World, ed. Peter Berger and Richard Neuhaus (New York: Seabury, 1976), pp. 99-125.

11. Webber, Common Roots, pp. 30-33.

12. Quebedeaux, The Young Evangelicals, pp. 39-40.

13. Mouw, "New Alignments," pp. 108-11.

14. Guth, "Evangelical Right," p. 3.

15. See, for example, R. Stephen Warner, "Theoretical Barriers to the Understanding of Evangelical Christianity," Sociological Analyses 40 (Spring 1979): 1-9; and Robert Johnston, Evangelicals at an Impasse (Atlanta: John Knox Press, 1979), p. 3.

16. George Gallup, Jr., "Divining the Devout: The Polls and Religious Belief," Public Opinion 4 (April-May 1981): 20; and Lipset and Raab, "Election and Evangelicals," p. 25.

17. Joseph Fichter and George Maddox, "Religion in the South, Old and New," in The South in Continuity and Change, ed. John McKinney and Edgar Thompson (Durham, N.C.: Duke University Press, 1965), p. 359.

18. John Shelton Reed, The Enduring South: Subcultural Persistence in a Mass Society (Lexington, Mass.: D. C. Heath, Lexington Books, 1972), chap. 6; and Samuel S. Hill, Jr., The South and the North in American Religion (Athens: University of Georgia Press, 1980), p. 138.

19. Dwight Dorough, The Bible Belt Mystique (Philadelphia: Westminster Press, 1974), p. 191; and Reed, The Enduring South, p. 68.

20. George Gallup, Jr., The Gallup Poll: Public Opinion 1980 (Wilmington, Del.: Scholarly Resources, 1981), p. 188.

21. Dorough, The Bible Belt Mystique, p. 199.

22. Fichter and Maddox, "Religion in the South," p. 383; and Reed, The Enduring South, pp. 69-74.

23. Specifically, as was mentioned above, Gallup has utilized a question tapping respondents' concern for encouraging others to believe in Jesus Christ, while the operational measure employed in this study includes an item tapping the importance of religion in the respondent's life. In addition, it should be noted that the closed-ended responses associated with the item tapping respondents' perceptions of the authority of the Bible differ slightly between the Gallup and Michigan studies.

24. See the discussion and analysis presented in Charles Hadley, "Survey Research and Southern Politics: The Implication of Data Management," Public Opinion Quarterly 45 (Fall 1981): 393-401.

25. Lipset and Raab, "Election and Evangelicals," p. 26.

26. Leo Dreedger, "Doctrinal Belief: A Major Factor in the Differential Perception of Social Issues," Sociological Quarterly 15 (Winter 1974): 66.

27. Guth, "Evangelical Right," pp. 13-14.

28. Albert Menendez, "Religion at the Polls, 1980," Church of State 34 (December 1980): 18; and Lipset and Raab, "Election and Evangelicals," p. 30.

29. Lipset and Raab, "Election and Evangelicals," p. 30.

30. While Reagan's Evangelical credentials are less impressive than Carter's, there is no denying that Reagan sought to label himself as an Evangelical Christian in the 1980 election.

31. James Fairbanks, "The Evangelical Right and America's Civil Religion" (Paper presented at the 1981 Annual Meeting of the Western Political Science Association, Denver, March 26).

32. Robert Salisbury and Michael MacKuen, "On the Study of Party Realignment," Journal of Politics 43 (May 1981): 525.

33. Susan Howell, "The Behavioral Component of Changing Partisanship," American Politics Quarterly 8 (July 1980): 279-302.

34. For example, a paper presented at a recent meeting of a regional political science association operationally defined <u>Fundamentalists</u> as those who expressed such denominational affiliations as Christian Reformed, Reformed Church in America, Church of the Latter Day Saints, Mormons, and United Church of Christ.

35. For example, differences in emphasis upon cultural separation versus cultural involvement as well as differences in emphasis upon social welfare vis-à-vis spiritual welfare have important political ramifications.

3

THE EFFECTS OF
EVANGELICALISM ON
SOUTHERN BLACK AND
WHITE POLITICAL ATTITUDES
AND VOTING BEHAVIOR

Jerry Perkins
Donald Fairchild
Murray Havens

From an impressionistic point of view, religion appears to have been an important part of the conduct of the 1980 elections. Evangelical spokesmen were on the offensive and the thrust of their activity was clear at least in broad outline. Media-based ministries such as the Moral Majority wanted a return to what they saw as long-deserted moral standards in U.S. politics and government. Their political objects varied from the rather specific congressional "hit lists" to a less clear but still obvious preference for the Reagan presidential candidacy. Whether from the glowing connection between Reagan and the Evangelicals at religious rallies or from the attack on various aspects of the Carter presidency, the message was obvious. It was to be a Republican year for the more fundamentalist religious leadership in the country.[1]

The role of religion in citizens' voting decisions is less clear than the partisan activity of the religious leadership. While the core political strategy of the Fundamentalist Right is to mobilize the faithful into a cohesive and punishing voting bloc, much commentary during the campaign and immediately following the election suggested that at least in presidential politics no such cohesion existed.[2] In fact, there was some evidence that Evangelicals were more pro-Carter than the average voter.[3]

There are problems in the assessments of Evangelical voting behavior in 1980. First, much of the periodic literature spoke of the Evangelicals as a unified group, which it is not. Not only are there internal disputes over the role of religion in politics, but there is the factor of race as well.[4] Black Americans are overwhelmingly Protestant, and any reasonable guess would count their numbers as high in the nondenominational categories often called Evangelical or Fundamentalist. Blacks are perhaps the most resistant group to conservative appeals, at least in national party politics where their overwhelming Democratic liberalism is well known. In effect, to ignore race while examining religious Fundamentalism may well obscure opposite tendencies between blacks and whites. It is a matter of "ethnoreligious" lines rather than simply religious belief. Any estimation of the attitudes and behavior of Evangelicals, therefore, should be made with the proper race controls.

Another problem relates to 1980 voting behavior in the light of long-run trends. First, the academic literature, while not specifying Evangelical groups, does document lower voting-turnout rates among Protestants than among other religious groups, and voter registration drives of the organized groups seem to be based on the notion that the faithful have been more concerned with the afterlife than with current secular events.[5] Did in fact Evangelicals surge to the polls in a higher number than expected?

This chapter seeks to assess the overall political contribution of white and black Evangelicals in the region where their numbers are highest, the South. Survey data from the University of Michigan's Center for Political Studies are used to compare religious and racial factors in four areas: social characteristics, attitudes, voting turnout, and vote direction in 1976 and 1980.

POLITICAL AND RELIGIOUS CLEAVAGES: THE POTENTIAL OF EVANGELICAL POLITICS IN THE SOUTH

While the doctrine of church-state separation is strong in the United States, there are numerous perspectives on the interaction between religion and politics. In the broadest cultural sense the "civil religion" permeates all of the country's society.[6] In a related way, the structure of political myth can be viewed metaphorically from a religious perspective.[7] Given the obvious intertwining of the two, some are concerned with the proper role of religious values in political life.[8] As for political behavior, the use of religion by presidents can be analyzed,[9] or the symbols of religion as they appear in presidential elections can be scrutinized.[10] In addition, research on voting behavior has been concerned with the role of religion in electoral choice from the earliest works.[11]

How might religious beliefs be manifested in political behavior and how might they contribute to current political cleavages? In elections religion can be important in two ways. First, there is the degree to which voting behavior is affected by the religious group memberships of both candidates and voters, as was the case in the 1960 election. In this type of election, the analyst is interested in the inclinations of Catholics to vote for their coreligionist candidate and the inclinations of Protestants to vote against that candidate. In 1960 a significant number of southern Protestant Democrats did defect to the Republicans because of John F. Kennedy's religion. [12] Perhaps Jimmy Carter's first presidential race in 1976 could be viewed similarly. It is thought by some that his coreligionists in the South and the Midwest gave him a disproportionate number of votes, [13] although analysis of national survey data actually shows Carter with slightly less than the expected vote among Protestants in general. [14] The latter analysis, however, may underestimate the coreligionist vote because Protestant denominational membership may not exactly correspond to the born-again group and race. This was not controlled for in the analysis and could be a confounding factor as well.

Second, religion might affect political choice through the influence of religious attitudes on political attitudes. This seems to be the dominant theme in 1980. Carter's born-again Evangelicism may have made him unique as a coreligionist in 1976, but by 1980 the political landscape had significantly changed. Not only was the question of candidate religion muted by the announced born-again religious values of all three major candidates, but the thrust of the religious Right was on issue evaluation as it related to doctrinaire religious thought. The central question for the analyst of politics and religion in this case is, What are the political value implications of Evangelical or Fundamentalist doctrine?

One theoretical tack is to relate religious doctrine to broadly viewed economic conservatism. In the case of Protestant Fundamentalism, for example, Everett L. Perry claims that economic conservatism appeals to Fundamentalists, some of whom have succeeded in terms of wealth and some of whom have not.

> Both major strands of economic conservatism—that which arises from the desire to maintain an attained economic advantage, and that which resists change on the basis of tradition, despite lack of economic advantage—are congenial to the fundamentalist ethic. [15]

So even the poor among the Fundamentalists would presumably support traditional economic inequalities and perhaps align themselves with Republican party politics. The evidence for this view, however, is not strong. Other observers have attempted to test Perry's basic assumptions by dividing survey respondents between liberal and conservative types of Protestantism, hypothesizing that membership in one or the other corresponds to political/economic ideology, but little effect has been shown. [16] More extensive elaborations by sociologists refine the basic hypothesis by making political conservatism and/or Republican party identification contingent on attending a conservative church and by making liberalism and/or Democratic identification contingent on attending a liberal church. [17] However, reanalysis of this data shows no significant effect. [18] To further complicate the matter, one longitudinal analysis shows opposite effects of church attendance between regions, with high attendance producing high Democratic identification in the South—although the regional distinctions are declining over time. [19]

Perhaps there is less than comprehensive correspondence between religious and political doctrines. The work of historians on voting in the nineteenth century emphasizes the existence of sociocultural lines of cleavage elicited by issues that were primarily social rather than economic (for example, prohibition). It is argued that pietistic Protestants of the time were particularly inclined to conservatism because of such issues and because of their resistance to new religious ethnics (Catholics, primarily) that represented the opposite cultural values. [20] In terms of party, pietistic Protestants developed deep Republican roots, but the second major political fault line of the day, sectionalism, operated in a different way to throw southern Protestants into the Democratic party. The election of 1896 saw the victory of McKinley and the domination of economic over social issues, thus bringing that particular alignment to an end.

This episode of U.S. history illustrates the ebb and flow of types of political issues that can potentially elicit religious cleavage. There are also crosscutting forces, primarily economic and racial (or sectional) in nature. In the non-South, Catholics and Protestants have retained some of the earlier division into the twentieth century, but now more often than not texts on opinion will say that class factors account for much of the political variation between the groups. [21] Southern white Protestants have been Democratic, because of regionalism, of course, but forces of economic modernization and social change now offer the Republican party as a legitimate alternative. [22] Even with declining regional differences, however, class factors may well keep many Fundamentalist southern white Protestants in the Democratic party if their status is low and if economic issues are dominant. Blacks, originally loyal to the party of Lincoln, have by now for economic and racial reasons become the most solid group in the Democratic coalition.

The potential of sociocultural issues for religious voting behavior is indirectly illustrated by more recent studies on state policies. While many areas of economic policy are related to economic factors in the United States, [23] one study finds an association between religion and state policies on liquor and gambling. [24] Using aggregate data, this study shows that intolerance of liquor and gambling is directly related to the size of a state's Fundamentalist Protestant population and that this relationship holds even where economic development is controlled. In many states, of course, such issues may never emerge because of overwhelming odds against them, and other issues may therefore underlie the partisan voting cleavages. But clearly under some conditions the moral issues could constitute a major and persistent fault line in politics. The emergence of moral issues could crosscut economic cleavages and draw poor whites and blacks from liberal to more conservative coalitions.

From the perspective of national politics, some observers think the decade of the 1960s and the early 1970s produced the circumstances for a set of political cleavages based on morality. From the civil rights movement to radical students, the challenges of feminism, school prayer, and abortion, the 1960s and 1970s represented a political watershed. In addition, the emergence of varying life-styles related to dress, manners, and consumption of drugs and pornography raised serious challenges to traditional behavioral standards. These emergent trends did not square neatly with the New Deal alliances, which were primarily economic in origin. Beginning in the late 1960s a spate of commentary took much notice of the possibilities surrounding the "social" issue.[25] The book Religion and the New Majority, which sought to chronicle moral issues and to anticipate the future, is probably the most explicit and partisan work on the subject.[26] Its authors identified the moral problems of the day and suggested new alliances between economic conservatives of the Republican party and Fundamentalist religious conservatives on social issues.

What could be more fertile ground for a religious revival, particularly an ethnocentric one, than the South? The region's Protestant numbers are large, especially in terms of neo-Fundamentalists. While the economic conservatism of southern whites may have been overestimated historically, racism has certainly been evident among the dominant white population and traditional values on social issues might have a chance to flourish here more than elsewhere.[27] There is, of course, variation in the modern South. The region is new in many senses. Perhaps the most significant change is the addition of the black population to the electorate. Also important is the immigration of non-Southerners.

Emergent diversity in the South provides the logic of this inquiry. Basic political changes have responded to social and economic alterations in the region. While the proportion of Democrats has dropped sharply in the postwar South, they still constitute the majority.[28] Jimmy Carter's 1980 vote total fell far below the partisan norm, of course. To what extent was this the result of Carter's born-again brethren defecting from their traditional party? Are defectors the results of social issues? Or, perhaps, have southern Evangelicals undergone a more fundamental political transformation and converted to Independence or Republicanism? To what degree must these queries also address the question of race?

METHODS AND DATA

The most important methodological problem is in identifying Evangelicals or Fundamentalists. Neither term closely corresponds to organized denominations, although of course there are overlaps (for example, Southern Baptists). Rather, the terms are more representative of what might be called popular religion.[29] They exist as movements both in and out of churches and represent a state of mind more than formal membership. Also, distinctions can be made between Evangelicalism and Fundamentalism. The latter is thought to be distinctively antiintellectual, more reactionary on theological doctrine, and perhaps more appealing to lower-status rural residents.[30] The available data do not allow making distinctions between the two, but they do permit examination of points that are shared. Generally, both emphasize the acceptance of Jesus Christ as one's savior, the Bible as God's written word, and the spreading of the Gospel.

In measuring survey respondents' attitudes toward these subjects, we move from a simple classification of denominational types to a psychologically based indicator. The 1980 presidential election study conducted by the Center for Political Studies (CPS) allows this through an examination of responses to four questions: (1) whether religion is important in one's life, (2) how much guidance religion provides in day-to-day living (some, quite a bit, or a great deal), (3) whether one has been born again, and (4) a question on the Bible (four responses ranging from a literalist interpretation to the view that the Bible is irrelevant today).[31] A simple dichotomous index was created. To be classified as Evangelical, a respondent had to say that religion is important, that it offers quite a bit or a great deal of guidance, that one has been born again, and that the Bible is literally the word of God. The second category, which will be termed non-Evangelical, is composed of those who failed to give the Evangelical response to any of the four items. The two-part index was then combined with race to produce a four-part classification of religion and race. The classification seems to have a great deal of face validity, but construct validity is also established by relating the distribution of this basic indicator to objective church membership and to church attendance. The only major weakness in the index is the absence of a direct question on spreading the gospel, or "witnessing for Christ." Clearly, those who witness would surely consider religion as providing guidance to their everyday lives, but not all those for whom religion is important would necessarily be witnesses for Christ. To some degree, then, the Evangelical category may overstate the actual numbers.

A second methodological concern is in determining whether or not Evangelicals exhibited more involvement in the 1980 campaign than usual. The problem arises because comparable questions on Evangelicalism were absent in earlier surveys. This particular issue is treated in two ways. First, the four religious categories are compared in terms of interest in and involvement with the 1980 campaign, and second, self-reports of voting turnout in past presidential contests are examined.

The 1980 CPS survey provides many issues and social indicators relevant to this study. It includes a series of the standard seven-point scales on economic concerns (for example, whether government should help people get jobs or leave them on their own) and social concerns (for example, whether women should be accorded equal status or be housewives). Additional relevant questions are not cast in the seven-point format. Included are questions on attitudes toward the Equal Rights Amendment and abortion. The general hypothesis is that Evangelicals are not distinct on economic issues but that they are more conservative than other religious groups on some social or cultural issues. Race, of course, is a complicating factor. Are black Evangelicals conservative on social issues? Insofar as the social domain includes popular assessments of minority-group rights, the casual observer would not expect to find similarities across race. But on other questions such as school prayer more favorable attitudes toward prayer may be found among both black and white Evangelicals than among the less religious members of both races. This distinction between religious and racial cleavages constitutes the basic focus of the analysis across all areas of concern.

PROFILE OF THE RELIGIOUS GROUPS

A total of 836 Southerners responded to all the religious questions and are classified in one of the four religion/race categories. Of the 720 whites, 25 percent (N = 183) provided perfect Evangelical responses. A significantly higher proportion of the blacks is scored similarly: of 116, 43 percent (N = 50) are placed in the Evangelical category.

If our measure of Evangelicalism is valid, the groups should be to some degree distinguished in terms of denominational preference. As Table 3.1 illustrates, this is in fact the case. Among both white and black Evangelicals there is a high incidence of neo-Fundamentalist memberships. Both racial groups classified as non-Evangelical are less likely to belong to Fundamentalist denominations than are Evangelicals. Generally, non-Evangelicals are more diverse in denominational preference than are Evangelicals. Among whites, 19 percent are Catholic; roughly 25 percent fall into both the neo-Fundamentalist and pietistic Protestant categories; 16 percent are Reformation-era

TABLE 3.1

Denominational Membership by Religion and Race
(in percent)

	White		Black	
	Evangelical*	Non-Evangelical	Evangelical*	Non-Evangelical
Protestant, general	6	4	0	1
Protestant, Reformation era (for example, Presbyterian, Lutheran, Episcopalian)	6	16	0	1
Protestant, pietistic (for example, Methodist, Christian, nonsouthern Baptist)	23	26	45	42
Neo-Fundamentalist (for example, Church of God, Church of Christ, Southern Baptist)	58	23	42	35
Nontraditional Christian (for example, Unitarian, Unity, Mormon)	0	2	2	0
Catholic	7	19	10	12
Jewish	0	1	0	0
Eastern Orthodox	0	1	0	0
Other	0	1	0	0
None	1	7	2	9
(N)	(180)	(508)	(66)	(50)

*Percentages in this column do not always total 100 because of rounding error.

Note: In this table the level of statistical significance is at .05 or better.

Source: Compiled by the authors from Center for Political Studies data.

TABLE 3.2

Selected Characteristics of Racial and Religious Groups
(in percent)

	White		Black	
	Evangelical	Non-Evangelical	Evangelical	Non-Evangelical
Attending church every week	53	17	37	25
Female	65	52	68	59
Grew up on farm or in country	43	26	71	39
Mean age	47	42	48	38
More than a high school education	29	46	8	20
Yearly family income above $19,999	46	62	24	19
Identify as Democrats	51	40	73	75

Note: In this table the level of statistical significance is .05 or better.

Source: Compiled by the authors from Center for Political Studies data.

Protestant; and 7 percent profess no membership. Black non-Evangelicals are less diverse than their white counterparts, but are distributed somewhat more widely than Evangelical blacks. The index of religious Evangelicalism is given further support by the part of Table 3.2 that reports church attendance among the four groups. A majority of respondents in the most religious white group say they attend church every week; only 17 percent of other whites do the same. Although black Evangelicals claim weekly attendance less often than whites, a higher proportion of their number do so than other blacks (37 percent to 25 percent).

The balance of Table 3.2 illustrates similar patterns of difference across religious categories on selected social characteristics. The proportion of females is high among both racial groups with high religious commitment (roughly two-thirds in each case). Evangelicals more than others report growing up in a rural setting. Similarly, the mean ages of both white and black Evangelicals are higher than those of the other two groups. On education and income there are both racial and religious differences. As might be expected, whites rank significantly higher than blacks in terms of both educational achievement and family income. However, intragroup comparisons show Evangelicals among both races to be less well educated than their non-Evangelical counterparts. With respect to income, the same generalization is true only of whites; black Evangelicals have slightly higher income than other blacks.

The only indicator in Table 3.2 that clearly shows large racial difference and low religious difference is political partisanship. Roughly three in four blacks of both religious categories identify as Democrats. Whites' identification with the traditional party of the South is much lower. A majority of Evangelicals still consider themselves Democrats; a slightly lower proportion (40 percent) of non-Evangelicals do.

POLITICAL ATTITUDES OF EVANGELICALS

The political attitudes that voters carry to the polls are of potential importance in determining how the vote is cast. In the case of religious Fundamentalists, the common notion is that they carry a type of conservative creed, at least with respect to noneconomic issues. Certainly the social and demographic characteristics of the Evangelicals under consideration would lead to an expectation of social conservatism. Their lower education and rural upbringing may inculcate more resistance to modifications of longstanding cultural practices. And, to some degree, the disproportionate number of women might also bias Evangelicals' responses in favor of more traditional standards.

A total of 15 issues were selected from the CPS study. Some are economic in nature, some are social, some are racial, and some are not easily classifiable. In comparing the religious and racial bases of the responses, a multivariate technique such as discriminate function would be ideal. However, methodological considerations as well as clarity of presentation make it necessary to present each issue one at a time as displayed in Table 3.3.[32] To give some order to the results, the questions are divided into three categories: those where racial differences are greater than religious differences (part A), those where religious differences are greater than racial differences (part B), and those where there are no significant differences (part C). Questions appearing in part C were insignificant by the chi-square measure of statistical significance. Placement in parts A and B is determined by a very crude method of numerical comparison. An average conservatism score for the two racial groups (irrespective of religion) is determined. The black average is then subtracted from the white average. The procedure for religion is the same (race is ignored): the score of non-Evangelicals is subtracted from the score of Evangelicals. The two results are compared. If the magnitude of the racial difference is greater than the magnitude of the religious difference, the question is classified in part A; if the reverse occurs it is classified in part B. Finally, within each part the questions are ordered from greatest difference to least difference.

On eight of the 15 issues variations between the races are greater than variations between the religious classifications. Two of these eight are economic in nature: government job guarantees and the question of whether government should reduce expenditures and services. On both, whites of both religious groups are clearly more conservative than their black counterparts. Three issues are racial in nature: government help for minority groups, the correct speed of civil rights progress, and school busing to achieve integration. On all three whites are more conservative than blacks, but on busing there is a matter of degree of conservatism because all four groups exhibit majorities against it. An item on the Equal Rights Amendment (ERA) clearly reflects one dominant social view of the day. Whites are significantly more likely to oppose the ERA than are blacks. Whites also exhibit more conservatism than blacks in providing higher support for defense spending (although all four groups provide majorities) and for nuclear power (although all four groups provide less than majorities).

Differences among religious groups appear where expected on three current social issues. Evangelicals more than others oppose legalized abortion and support prayer in public schools. On a forced-choice question about whether women should remain in the home or have equal roles with men, Evangelicals are also clearly the more

TABLE 3.3

Conservative Responses on Selected Issues by Race and Religion

	Percent	(N)
A. Issues on which racial differences are greater than religious differences*		
Government let each person get ahead on own (rather than help)		
White Evangelicals	57	(154)
White Non-Evangelicals	61	(421)
Black Evangelicals	15	(41)
Black Non-Evangelicals	24	(55)
Civil rights people have been pushing too fast		
White Evangelicals	58	(80)
White Non-Evangelicals	39	(218)
Black Evangelicals	4	(27)
Black Non-Evangelicals	10	(30)
Oppose ERA		
White Evangelicals	61	(148)
White Non-Evangelicals	37	(475)
Black Evangelicals	14	(41)
Black Non-Evangelicals	18	(49)
Minority groups should help themselves (rather than depend on government)		
White Evangelicals	59	(155)
White Non-Evangelicals	58	(487)
Black Evangelicals	36	(39)
Black Non-Evangelicals	28	(57)
We should keep children in neighborhood schools (as opposed to busing)		
White Evangelicals	92	(30)
White Non-Evangelicals	89	(225)
Black Evangelicals	67	(24)
Black Non-Evangelicals	52	(27)
Greatly increase defense spending		
White Evangelicals	82	(119)
White Non-Evangelicals	77	(359)

	Percent	(N)
Greatly increase defense spending (continued)		
Black Evangelicals	62	(29)
Black Non-Evangelicals	55	(36)
Government should reduce expenditures, provide fewer services		
White Evangelicals	36	(111)
White Non-Evangelicals	41	(331)
Black Evangelicals	6	(31)
Black Non-Evangelicals	17	(41)
Build more nuclear plants		
White Evangelicals	33	(108)
White Non-Evangelicals	44	(359)
Black Evangelicals	24	(33)
Black Non-Evangelicals	21	(43)

B. Issues on which religious differences are greater than racial differences*

	Percent	(N)
Abortion never permitted, or only in case of rape, incest, danger to mother		
White Evangelicals	76	(131)
White Non-Evangelicals	32	(377)
Black Evangelicals	65	(37)
Black Non-Evangelicals	59	(47)
Women's place is in the home (as opposed to having equal role with men)		
White Evangelicals	34	(80)
White Non-Evangelicals	19	(226)
Black Evangelicals	54	(26)
Black Non-Evangelicals	24	(29)
Allow prayer in public schools		
White Evangelicals	94	(176)
White Non-Evangelicals	74	(444)
Black Evangelicals	94	(48)
Black Non-Evangelicals	86	(51)

(continued)

TABLE 3.3 (continued)

	Percent	(N)

C. Issues on which there are no significant group differences

Reduce inflation, even if unemployment goes up

	Percent	(N)
White Evangelicals	33	(77)
White Non-Evangelicals	30	(243)
Black Evangelicals	23	(21)
Black Non-Evangelicals	29	(35)

Taxes should be cut by 20 percent or more

White Evangelicals	61	(104)
White Non-Evangelicals	61	(335)
Black Evangelicals	57	(19)
Black Non-Evangelicals	57	(26)

Big mistake to try to get along with Russia

White Evangelicals	40	(116)
White Non-Evangelicals	41	(349)
Black Evangelicals	36	(22)
Black Non-Evangelicals	36	(36)

Relax environmental protection to obtain more energy

White Evangelicals	48	(113)
White Non-Evangelicals	49	(360)
Black Evangelicals	48	(27)
Black Non-Evangelicals	51	(37)

*A classification of parts A and B of this table is based on very crude comparisons of race and religious categories. If the average difference on conservatism between the races is greater than the average difference between the religious classifications, the question is placed in part A; if the reverse is true, the question is placed in part B.

Note: In this table the level of statistical significance is .05 or better.

Source: Compiled by the authors from Center for Political Studies data.

conservative group. While religious differences are greatest on all three issues, it should be noted that there are overwhelming majorities among all four groups for prayer in the schools.

Items on which there are no significant group differences include two economic questions, one international question, and one environmental question. All four groups are roughly equal in not supporting antiinflation measures where unemployment would rise. A majority of each of the four groups, however, do support tax cuts of 20 percent or more. With respect to the Soviet Union there is little intergroup variation, with somewhat less than half of all classifications saying it is a "big mistake to try to get along with Russia." Finally, all groups divide roughly evenly on whether environmental protection ought to be relaxed to obtain more energy.

Viewed broadly, racial differences are predominant. On all but three issues—treatment of women, school prayer, and abortion—whites are more conservative than blacks. While religious differences are less important than racial ones, the general trend across all questions is for Evangelicals to be conservative. Among whites only two issues—government expenditures and government help for individuals—show a reversal, with Evangelicals being more liberal. Among blacks the same two exceptions prevail, as well as two more. Black Evangelicals are slightly more liberal on the ERA and on the civil rights issue than are black non-Evangelicals.

POLITICAL INVOLVEMENT OF EVANGELICALS

Presidential contests provide opportunities for the major parties to focus on a variety of strategies designed to attract a maximum number of voters in each state. While the most obvious goal is to secure each state's electoral votes for the party candidate, a long-term objective is to strengthen the party's coalition through mobilization and/or conversion of the electorate.[33] Mobilization was given a high priority among the strategies employed in 1980, and it is appropriate here to examine its utilization among the religious constituency within the South. Mobilization is a particularly attractive strategy among southern voters because of patterns of voting behavior established in past decades. These patterns emphasize the propensity of southern white voters to display little loyalty to the national party in most of the elections since 1948.

The social, demographic, and political characteristics of Evangelicals suggest comparatively little involvement with politics in general. Their predominantly lower status and female gender are characteristics associated with less participation,[34] as is their Democratic identification.[35] There is one exception, however. Evangelicals' high rate of church attendance may act in an offsetting direction.

Religiosity as measured by church attendance has been shown to be positively related to voter turnout. [36]

The data provide mixed answers to the question of whether religious Fundamentalism activated the interest of the faithful in the 1980 elections. There are no statistically significant differences between ethnoreligious groups in terms of thinking the election to be important, nor are there group differences on monitoring the election on radio and television (see Table 3.4). Interestingly, however, blacks in both religious groups are more inclined than their white counterparts to say that they "care who wins." And blacks generally are less likely to read about the election in magazines than are whites; the latter are divided on religious lines, with white Evangelicals far less likely than other whites to follow the election in print. Both racial and religious differences are likely to be the result of varying educational levels.

The acid test of the mobilization thesis, of course, is actual voter turnout. While the common assumption is that 1980 brought an Evangelical surge, it is obvious that Jimmy Carter's presence on the ballot four years earlier could have also attracted some attention. To gain a larger perspective on both the 1976 and 1980 elections, one can first examine respondents' recall of voting over the entire course of their lives. This is illustrated in Table 3.5. Both white groups report a higher incidence of voting than blacks. Although the accuracy of such broad recall questions may not entirely be trusted, the evidence is certainly consistent with what one would guess to be the case with respect to race. Southern black voting was not backed by the force of federal law until 1965, and many of the black respondents could not have voted in their early years.

Table 3.5 also illustrates some religious differences, but such variance is the opposite across racial groups. For whites, non-Evangelicals are more likely than other whites to report a high incidence of previous voting. Among blacks, Evangelicals have a longer personal history of involvement in voting than other blacks. This intergroup variance suggests that the religious experience might vary across ethnic lines. It is obvious to the observer of black politics that the church has been a primary institutional source of activism, while the white church has been perhaps somewhat less worldly.

The potential rise of political activism among white Evangelicals is the crucial aspect of this investigation. First was the born-again candidacy of Carter in 1976; then came the challenge to Carter by the religious Right in 1980. Did either bring a surge? Table 3.6 provides a partial answer. While white Evangelicals do report less involvement than other whites over the course of their lives, in 1976 there are no significant white differences in turnout, with two of three recalling a vote. In 1980 the non-Fundamentalists stay at about the

TABLE 3.4

Interest in the 1980 Presidential Election by Religion and Race
(in percent)

	White		Black	
	Evan-gelical	Non-Evan-gelical	Evan-gelical	Non-Evan-gelical
Think elections important*	43	43	46	36
Care who wins	51	57	74	76
Listen to polls on radio*	50	47	40	49
Read polls in magazines	24	45	12	9
See polls on television*	87	89	96	86

*Percentage differences are not statistically significant.

Source: Compiled by the authors from Center for Political Studies data.

TABLE 3.5

Recall of Voting Turnout in Previous Elections by Religion and Race
(in percent)

	White		Black	
	Evan-gelical	Non-Evan-gelical	Evan-gelical	Non-Evan-gelical
All	36	45	26	11
Most	26	25	29	22
Some	23	15	26	29
None	14	15	18	38
Total	99	100	100	100
(N)	(118)	(327)	(38)	(45)

Note: In this table the level of statistical significance is .05 or better.

Source: Compiled by the authors from Center for Political Studies data.

TABLE 3.6

Voting Turnout in the 1976 and 1980 Presidential Elections by Religion
and Race
(in percent)

	White		Black	
	Evan-gelical	Non-Evan-gelical	Evan-gelical	Non-Evan-gelical
1976*	67	66	67	42
1980*	77	67	68	63

*Percentage differences are not statistically significant.

Source: Compiled by the authors from Center for Political Studies data.

same level, but the religious white group rises ten points. For blacks, the opposite trend prevails again. In 1976 religiously committed blacks voted at the same rate as whites but far above other blacks (67 percent as opposed to 42 percent), and in 1980 black non-Evangelicals increased their turnout rate to 63 percent from a previous rate of 42 percent. Looking across all four groups, in 1980 the highest reported turnout is among white Evangelicals. The differences are not large (and not statistically significant at the .05 level), but in combination with the larger recall evidence they do suggest a modicum of support for the notion that whites could have been politicized in the most recent electoral period.

VOTE DIRECTION AMONG EVANGELICALS

Given the background characteristics, levels of involvement, and attitude distributions, the crucial question becomes, To what degree are there religious and racial bases of the vote? A rather definitive answer is suggested in Figure 3.1, which displays the Democratic vote for the 1976 and 1980 presidential elections by religion and race. In both elections the proportion of blacks voting for Carter is extremely high, exceeding 90 percent in three of the four entries. Whites, on the other hand, show below a majority Democratic status in both years. The commitment of all four groups to Carter falls between 1976 and 1980. While the level of black support is high in both elections, black Evangelicals drop from 96 percent to 88 percent in support for Carter. Starting from a lower Democratic vote in 1976 (44 percent), white Evangelicals drop to 37 percent. However, the category showing the greatest decline in Democratic voting is non-Evangelical whites. They fall from 48 percent to 32 percent. Among whites, then, the relationship between religion as it is measured here and the two votes is reversed over time. Relatively speaking, Carter did better among non-Evangelical whites in 1976 and worse in 1980. Part of the decline is no doubt related to Anderson's candidacy. Anderson received 5 percent of the white non-Evangelical vote, which was his largest draw from any of the four groups.

The characteristics of both the black vote and the vote for Anderson limit our ability to say anything further. Anderson simply did not garner enough votes in the South to provide a sufficient numerical base for confident generalization. Similarly, the decline in black voting is small; the overwhelming aspect of black voting is its Democratic nature. In most respects neither the low incidence of Anderson votes nor the black bloc vote are surprising. What may be more unusual are the two white categories. Among the latter there is no dramatic line of cleavage suggesting differential responses across religious groups to current politics.

FIGURE 3.1

Percentages of Each Group Voting Democratic in 1976 and 1980
by Religion and Race

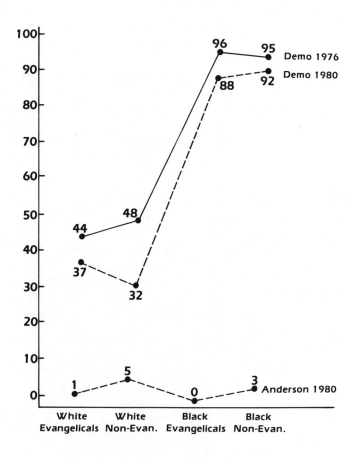

Do these findings mean that social conservatism played no role in determining the southern white vote? Not necessarily. While a line of cleavage may not exist, both Evangelical and non-Evangelical groups may divide presidential votes in such a way that social conservatives are disproportionately inclined to vote for Reagan. That is, Evangelicals are not the only social conservatives in the white population, as is illustrated by the previous discussion of attitudes. In effect, Evangelical conservatives could combine with other conservatives.

To test more directly the effects of social conservatism among whites, seven issues were combined to form an index, which was run against the presidential votes in 1976 and 1980 (Anderson is omitted in 1980).[37] The index is moderately related to the inclination to be Evangelical (Gamma = .40). For a comparative benchmark, three of the economic issues were combined.[38] The economic index is not significantly related to Evangelicalism (Gamma = -.01).

Dichotomized versions of the two indexes are related to the two presidential votes in 1976 and 1980, with conservatives of either kind being less likely to vote Democratic (see Figure 3.2). However, two dominant features of these relationships bear directly on an understanding of the data. First, social conservatism is only weakly associated with the vote in either year; economic conservatism, by comparison, is rather strongly related to the vote. Second, the vote for Carter is less among both liberals and conservatives in 1980 than in 1976. That is, all categories of the Democratic vote declined by 1980. In the case of the economic index, the decline among conservatives (21 points) is somewhat sharper than that among liberals (14 points), thus making the 1980 correlation (Gamma = .72) higher than that of 1976 (Gamma = .55). On the social index the decline is even across ideological groups, with the 1980 association (Gamma = .30) being roughly the same as that of 1976 (Gamma = .28).

These results illustrate only a mild effect of social issues, and apparently even their small influence is not primarily filtered through Evangelicalism. What the 1980 presidential election data do suggest is a set of factors that crosscut all categories such that Carter lost votes in a fairly uniform way. Because Carter was the incumbent, evaluations of his presidency might operate in such a way. While an exhaustive analysis of presidential evaluation is beyond the scope of this chapter, it is appropriate to touch upon a few findings that bear on Evangelicalism.

Popular evaluations of President Carter are strongly related to the vote (Gamma = .80), and on the whole white Southerners viewed him negatively, with 61 percent disapproving strongly or moderately of his performance. The economic index is related mildly to presidential evaluation (Gamma = .29), but the social index is not a signifi-

FIGURE 3.2

Percentages of Liberals and Conservatives Voting Democratic in
1976 and 1980 by Social/Racial and Economic Identification,
Whites Only

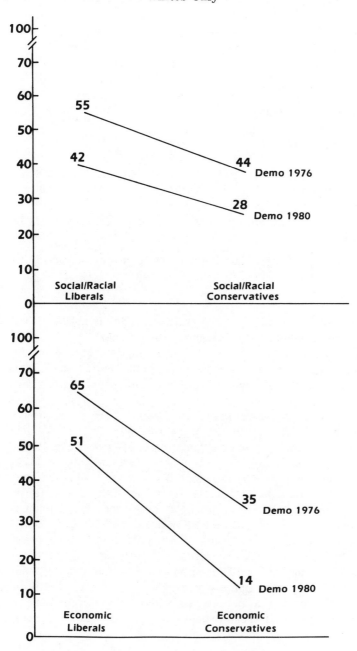

TABLE 3.7

Presidential Evaluation and the Vote by Religious Type, Whites Only
(in percent)

	Reagan	Carter	Total	(N)
Evangelical				
Approve strongly	6	94	100	(17)
Approve	35	65	100	(20)
Disapprove	95	5	100	(21)
Disapprove strongly	90	10	100	(41)
Non-Evangelical				
Approve strongly	14	86	100	(21)
Approve	32	68	100	(64)
Disapprove	67	33	100	(64)
Disapprove strongly	91	9	100	(116)

Note: In this table the level of statistical significance is .05 or better.

Source: Compiled by the authors from Center for Political Studies data.

cant correlate. Similarly, the religious index is not significantly related to presidential performance, and if there is a relationship it is the opposite of what Jerry Falwell might hope for: white Evangelicals approve of Carter's performance more than the non-Evangelicals! Positive assessments are offered by 42 percent of the former and by 37 percent of the latter.

The data increasingly call into question the assumption that religion was a significant factor in the 1980 election. This doubt is increased by examining other correlates of presidential evaluation. President Carter faced several notable crises during his term, most of which bore directly on citizens' assessment of his performance. These crises included the hostage crisis in Iran, the Soviet incursion into Afghanistan, inflation, unemployment, and energy issues. All are moderately strong predictors in presidential evaluation. In an analysis of these factors in the order given above, the gammas are .66, .40, .82, .65, and .62 (all are significant at the .001 level). Are white Evangelicals different on these determinants? Yes, mildly, but in the wrong direction. White Evangelicals are slightly more approving of presidential performance in these areas than are other religious groups in all areas except energy, although the associations

are weak (and insignificant at the . 05 level on Afghanistan and energy).
Two points should be made about these distributions. First, Evangelicals' slightly higher ratings are probably the result of their slightly
higher Democratic partisanship. Second, all groups have on balance
a negative view of the Carter presidency, either on specific crisis
items or on the general evaluation. It appears that presidential evaluations cut across both religious groups. This generalization is directly confirmed by comparing the vote with responses to the general
evaluation question, while controlling for religious categories among
whites (see Table 3. 7). The Carter vote falls across the evaluation
categories in a roughly similar fashion; and of course the Reagan
vote rises in the opposite fashion.

CONCLUSION

The most striking and obvious conclusion is that race remains
a significant factor—perhaps the most significant—in southern politics. While white and black Evangelicals may share many social
characteristics and some attitudes on social issues, their political
partisanship and their votes remain as divided as ever. Among
blacks the potential for morality-based appeals in campaigns appears
to be very limited as a vote-gathering device, at least as long as
race remains imprinted on national political coalitions. Given the
socioeconomic position of blacks in U. S. politics in general and in
southern politics in particular, one would not expect any near-term
alteration of these patterns. The racial experience, not the religious
experience, appears to be dominant for blacks. If anything, the religion of blacks may reinforce their political beliefs and behavior. Because blacks do contribute significant numbers of people to fundamentalist religion, to not control for race when interpreting the religious
bases of the vote would be to exaggerate the Democratic inclinations
of the born again.
Whites are more divided than blacks in terms of partisanship
and vote preference. The evidence that Evangelical religious pleas
had any effect on presidential voting among white Southerners, however, is marginal at best. Even if one were to concede that Evangelicals voted in higher numbers than usual in 1980, it appears the im-
pulse behind that vote was not primarily religious in nature. The social conservatism of white Evangelicals does offer a basis for mobilization under the right conditions. The question is, What are those
conditions? While it is difficult to state affirmatively what they might
be, the 1980 contest can be taken as evidence of what they are not.
An incumbent president faced with a diversity of problems not directly
related to the social or moral aspects of politics—as was the case

with Jimmy Carter—became the focal point in 1980. Evaluation of his performance on these primary problems simply overrode other considerations, with the result that both white religious groups were crosscut by their evaluations. Ronald Reagan may have been fairly representative of the social ideology of white Southerners, and he did garner a majority of their votes, but his success was perhaps more the result of Carter's failings than of ideological choice. In short, it may be more accurate to view the election as a plebiscite on the Carter administration.

In the short run, moral or social issues could have a decided influence on southern white votes, and there are enough moral liberals that a line of cleavage might form. In places where a politician becomes conspicuous on some social or moral issue (such as admitting to lustful desires in Playboy), attitudinal data imply strongly that the Evangelical vote could be as united as it (possibly) was outside of the South against senators like Culver of Iowa. This is not likely to happen frequently in southern state or local politics, given the rather pronounced overall conservative drift of the population on social and moral issues. Few politicians would risk being labeled liberal in the South, although of course some occasionally are against their will.

As for the long-term potential of religion in the South, data gathered from one point in time limit our ability to generalize, but there are some implications. Moral and social issues—particularly racial integration—have no doubt contributed to the overall decline in Democratic partisanship, and it appears that the greatest potential for long-run partisan change is among white Evangelicals. Yet they remain the most doggedly Democratic white group to date. Beyond racism, the social/cultural dimension does not seem to be capable of eliciting partisan change to the same degree as economic ideology, and on the latter Evangelicals are not particularly conservative. A cautious guess is that Evangelical political movements might sting a politician here or there but that members of the faith will not be driven entirely from their traditional Democratic loyalties. In fact, if racism diminishes, the lower status of many Evangelicals may well keep them in the Democratic party. Ultimately, then, economic considerations (which probably favor the Democrats) may be pitted against and override Republican moral exhortations in the battle for political souls.

NOTES

1. The literature covering the Evangelical Right and its politics is vast. For a fairly comprehensive listing, see Richard V. Pierard, Bibliography on the New Christian Right (Terre Haute, Ind.: Mimeo, 1981).

2. Seymour Lipset and Earl Raab, "The Election and the Evangelicals," Commentary 71 (March 1981): 25-31.

3. See, for example, the Gallup Poll data reported in "A Tide of Born-Again Politics," Newsweek, September 15, 1980, p. 36.

4. While there does seem to be a majority of Evangelicals writing from a right-wing perspective, there are dissenters. See, for example, Glenn E. Hinson, "Neo-Fundamentalism: An Interpretation and Critiques," Baptist History and Heritage 16 (April 1981): 33-42; and Dave Sproul, An Open Letter to Jerry Falwell (Tempe, Ariz.: Fundamental Baptist Press, 1979).

5. David B. Hill and Norman R. Luttbeg, Trends in American Electoral Behavior (Itasca, Ill.: F. E. Peacock, 1980), p. 91; and Herbert Asher, Presidential Elections and American Politics (Homewood, Ill.: Dorsey Press, 1976), p. 50.

6. Robert N. Bellah, "Civil Religion in America," in Religion in America, ed. William G. McLoughlin and Robert N. Bellah (Boston: Beacon, 1968).

7. Dan Nimmo and James Combs, Subliminal Politics (Englewood Cliffs, N.J.: Prentice-Hall, 1980).

8. Quentin L. Quade, "The Role of Religious Values in Political Judgement," Review of Politics 30 (October 1968): 415-27.

9. Arthur Hughes, "Amazin' Jimmy and a Mighty Fortress Was Our Teddy: Theodore Roosevelt and Jimmy Carter," Presidential Studies Quarterly 9 (Winter 1979): 80-82.

10. Bernard F. Donahue, "The Political Use of Religious Symbols: A Case Study of the 1972 Presidential Campaign," Review of Politics 37 (January 1975): 48-65.

11. Bernard R. Berelson, Paul F. Lazarsfeld, and William N. McPhee, Voting (Chicago: University of Chicago Press, 1954).

12. Philip E. Converse, Angus Campbell, Warren E. Miller, and Donald E. Stokes, "Stability and Change in 1960: A Reinstating Election," in Elections and the Political Order, ed. Angus Campbell, Philip E. Converse, Warren E. Miller, and Donald E. Stokes (New York: John Wiley & Sons, 1966), pp. 78-95.

13. Albert Menendez, Religion at the Polls (Philadelphia: Westminster Press, 1977), pp. 188, 195-97.

14. Arthur Miller, "Partisanship Reinstated? A Comparison of the 1972 and 1976 U.S. Presidential Elections," British Journal of Political Science 8 (April 1978): 129-52.

15. Everett L. Perry, "Socio-Economic Factors and American Fundamentalism," Review of Religious Research 1 (Summer 1959): 61-63.

16. Jerry Perkins, "Ideology in the South: Meaning and Bases among Masses and Elites," in Contemporary Southern Political Attitudes and Behavior, ed. Laurence W. Moreland, Tod A. Baker, and Robert P. Steed (New York: Praeger, 1982), pp. 6-23.

17. Benton Johnson, "Ascetic Protestantism and Political Preference in the Deep South," American Journal of Sociology 69 (January 1964): 359–66.

18. Gene F. Summers, Doyle P. Johnson, Richard L. Hough, and Kathryn A. Veatch, "Ascetic Protestantism and Political Preference: A Re-examination," Review of Religious Research 12 (Summer 1970): 17–25.

19. David Knoke, "Religious Involvement and Political Behavior: A Log-Linear Analysis of White Americans, 1952–1968," Sociological Quarterly 15 (Winter 1974): 51–65.

20. Paul Kleppner, The Third Electoral Era, 1853–1892: Parties, Voters and Political Cultures (Chapel Hill: University of North Carolina Press, 1978); and Richard Jensen, The Winning of the Midwest: Social and Political Conflict, 1888–1896 (Chicago: University of Chicago Press, 1971).

21. See, for example, Alan Monroe, Public Opinion in America (New York: Dodd, Mead, 1975).

22. See, among others, Jack Bass and Walter DeVries, The Transformation of Southern Politics (New York: Basic Books, 1976); and Laurence W. Moreland, Tod A. Baker, and Robert P. Steed, eds., Contemporary Southern Political Attitudes and Behavior (New York: Praeger, 1982).

23. Thomas R. Dye, Policies, Economics and the Public: Policy Outcomes in the American States (Chicago: Rand McNally, 1966).

24. David Fairbanks, "Religious Forces and 'Morality' Policies in the American States," Western Political Quarterly 30 (September 1975): 411–17.

25. Richard M. Scammon and Benjamin J. Wattenberg, The Real Majority, 3d ed. (New York: G. P. Putnam's Sons, 1970).

26. Lowell D. Streiker and Gerald S. Strober, Religion and the New Majority (New York: Association Press, 1972).

27. V. O. Key, Jr., Public Opinion and American Democracy (New York: Alfred A. Knopf, 1961).

28. Paul Allen Beck, "Partisan Dealignment in the Postwar South," American Political Science Review 71 (June 1977): 477–96; and Bruce A. Campbell, "Patterns of Change in the Partisan Loyalties of Native Southerners: 1952–1972," Journal of Politics 39 (August 1977): 730–61.

29. Peter W. Williams, Popular Religion in America (Englewood Cliffs, N.J.: Prentice-Hall, 1980).

30. Ibid., pp. 158–68; and Menendez, Religion at the Polls, pp. 138–46.

31. All questions used here are drawn from the 1980 election survey conducted by the Center for Political Studies, Institute for Social Research, University of Michigan. The CPS Codebook provides

detailed descriptions of all questions. For the four central questions, see the following variables: V1273, V1274, V1275, and V1276. Descriptions of the four are found on pp. 172 and 173 of the Codebook.

32. The 1980 study is composed of three panels conducted at various intervals throughout the election year. Panels are combined wherever possible to raise the number of respondents (the base N). In the case of attitudes, not all questions were asked of all respondents in all panels. This procedure, in combination with normal problems of missing data, severely reduces the N where we try to combine all issues in a multivariate analysis. This is particularly true of black respondents. Therefore, we have chosen to examine each question individually.

33. Angus Campbell, Philip E. Converse, Warren E. Miller, and Donald E. Stokes, The American Voter (New York: John Wiley & Sons, 1959).

34. Sidney Verba and Norman Nie, Participation in America (New York: Harper & Row, 1972).

35. Philip E. Converse, "The Concept of the Normal Vote," in Elections and the Political Order, ed. Campbell, Converse, Miller, and Stokes, pp. 9-39.

36. Theodore Macaluse and John Wanat, "Voting Turnout and Religiosity," Polity 12 (Fall 1979): 158-69.

37. The seven issues comprising the social index for use in the analysis of whites are V1222 (treatment of minority groups), V1248 (women's roles), V1270 (school busing), V1269 (speed of integration), V1234 (abortion), V1264 (equal rights amendment), and V1272 (school prayer).

38. The three issues are V1071 (inflation/unemployment), V1137 (service/spending), and V1177 (job guarantees).

4

RELIGION AND
POLITICAL ATTITUDES
IN THE URBAN SOUTH

Kenneth D. Wald
Michael B. Lupfer

For even a casual reader of the newspaper who encounters headlines about sectarian murders in Northern Ireland, the involvement of church officials in liberation movements around the globe, or the role of fundamentalist Islamic movements in many regimes of the Middle East, the connection between religion and politics seems inescapable. Despite this evidence, political scientists have traditionally been reluctant to appreciate the political significance of religious commitment. As Leon Epstein has noted, religious conflicts in politics have been treated as remnants of preindustrial politics, destined to wither away as economic modernization focused political conflict on issues related to distributive justice.[1] This forecast about the inevitable diminution of religious conflicts has now been called into question by research demonstrating the impressive survival power of religion as a political force.[2]

Though scholars have come to recognize the continuing political impact of religion, there is still considerable skepticism about the causal role of religious belief.[3] Thus observed links between religion and political behavior are usually attributed not to belief but rather to religion as a factor determining social status, membership in a subculture or interest group, or patterns of social interaction—models of influence that have little to do with the content of religious belief per se.[4] Although a few studies have suggested that religious beliefs may directly affect political outlooks,[5] the bulk of empirical evidence

We wish to thank those students at Memphis State University who assisted in this research. We are also grateful to Larry Petersen of the Department of Sociology at Memphis State University for several useful suggestions.

has cast doubt upon the political relevance of theology for the general population. [6]

The American South offers an excellent locale in which to search for the political impact of theology. As noted throughout this volume, commitment to Christian orthodoxy has been one of the most distinctive features of the South, a region where church membership and other forms of institutional religion have been noteworthy. The coincidence of conservative theology and conservative politics in the region lends a surface plausibility to hypotheses about links between religious and political outlooks. If religious belief does indeed dispose adherents to particular political perspectives, that relationship should be evident in the American South.

METHODS

In his influential review of attempts to link religious and political conservatism, Robert Wuthnow provided a stinging indictment of existing empirical research. [7] Previous studies were taken to task for (1) use of highly unrepresentative samples (usually college students), (2) failure to take into account the mediating effects of intervening variables, (3) overly simple models of religiosity, and (4) use of one-dimensional measures of sociopolitical attitudes. The study reported in this chapter was designed to provide findings that could withstand criticisms on these grounds. Thus an attempt was made to obtain interviews with a representative sample of the voting-age population of an entire community. The interview schedule probed respondents for information about background characteristics that might affect both the independent and dependent variables. Rather than adopting a simplistic definition, we sought to treat religion as a complex, multidimensional force. Similarly, the concept of conservatism was operationalized by constructing measures of sociopolitical attitudes across several different issue areas. Finally, we selected a method of statistical analysis that would allow for complex relationships among the various factors relevant to the problem. Although we have undoubtedly made at least our share of mistakes, this design does seem sufficient to meet Wuthnow's strictures.

The initial study design called for interviews with 300 residents of the Memphis Standard Metropolitan Statistical Area, with respondents to be selected through quota-sampling techniques. The target population was stratified on the basis of race, gender, age, and education according to the population parameters reported in the 1970 census. [8] The interviewers, upper-division students at Memphis State University, began fieldwork in the spring of 1981, and fieldwork continued until the end of the calendar year. [9] The interviews, which were tape-recorded with the permission of respondents, were coded by the interviewers and spot-checked by the authors. In the expanded sample, we obtained usable interviews with 359 respondents. [10] Although the principal concern was to maximize the variance in social characteristics of the sample, we are confident that the match between sample- and known-population parameters allows us to generalize the findings beyond the 359 respondents.

In its initial form (see Figure 4.1), our model posited both direct and indirect religious effects upon sociopolitical attitudes. The belief was that social characteristics would influence religious commitment and sociopolitical attitudes but would not account altogether for covariation of the key independent and dependent variables. This design required measurement of social background, several factors immediately antecedent to religious commitment, religious commitment, and sociopolitical attitudes.

Included as background factors were the four items defining the quotas: race, education, gender, and age. These factors have been repeatedly linked both to levels of religiosity[11] and to sociopolitical attitude orientations. [12] In addition to these four factors, it seemed essential to include a measure of socioeconomic status and thus respondents were asked about their current occupation and that of their parents. These data were then converted to scale scores on the Duncan socioeconomic index, [13] and each individual was assigned an occupational score for both current occupation and parental occupation. [14]

Another set of variables was constructed that were conceptualized as more proximate to religious commitment—current denomination, parent's denomination, and localism. The denominations were ordered on a scale according to their adherence to Christian orthodoxy. [15] Each respondent was asked to indicate the name of the church to which he or she currently belonged and the church to which his or her parents had belonged when the respondent was still living at home. The answers became the basis for coding current and childhood denomination, which in turn led to a score designed to reflect the degree of exposure to conservative theology. A measure of localism was included because of Wade Roof's suggestion that that phenomenon was strongly associated with both religious and political conservatism. [16] Although three items were included on the interview schedule, only two questions proved sufficiently reliable for the final localism index.

Our measurement of religiosity included most of the items initially included as part of the orthodoxy, ritualism, devotionalism, and experience indexes developed by Rodney Stark and Charles Glock as well as several items subsequently developed by other scholars. [17] Like many investigators who have entered this thicket of measurement, we did not find the degree of independence among these dimensions predicted by Stark and Glock. [18] Oblique factor analysis revealed

FIGURE 4.1

Hypothesized Causal Relationships

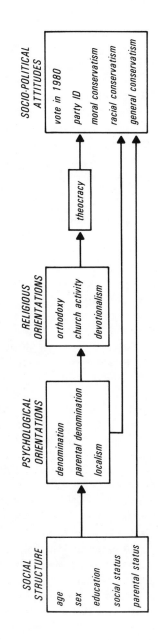

87

four clusters of attitudes, which were then combined into scales. The first factor, treated here as a measure of religious orthodoxy, picked up the orthodoxy items developed by Stark and Glock plus several items that conceptually seem to measure salvationism, religious experience, and other aspects of religion. However much we tried to force these additional items onto other scales, they insisted on forming a consistent, highly reliable index that included both orthodox belief and these additional items. As for Harold Quinley, it did not prove possible in our sample to separate commitment to the core items of orthodox Christianity from several theoretically independent items. [19] Bowing to the inevitable, we thus constructed an orthodoxy index with 14 items and a Cronbach's alpha of .84.

As noted above, there are aspects of religiosity other than belief that might have political implications. Several scholars have demonstrated that intensive involvement in the life of the institutional church, by exposing adherents to persuasive communication about social and political affairs, promotes a common political outlook among coreligionists. [20] We thus created a church-involvement scale based on reported frequency of attendance at worship and level of participation in other church activities. This measure was complemented by another variable that has been designated, following Stark and Glock, as an index of devotionalism. This measured the reported frequency of religious activity in the respondent's private life outside the church. It serves as another way of determining the salience of religious belief and the likelihood that religious perspectives will be applied to areas outside matters of theology.

As is well known to students of the subject, Fundamentalist religious belief has traditionally been associated with abstention from secular, especially political, affairs. [21] The application of Fundamentalist religious belief to worldly concerns would seem to depend upon the belief that it is proper for Christians to engage in political activity. We attempted to capture this disposition by including several items about the appropriateness of concerted Christian efforts in politics, and these items formed a cluster in the factor analysis. The resulting index, labeled theocracy, measures the respondent's approval for organized Christian involvement in the political process. [22] Theoretically, it is seen as a crucial link translating conservative religious orientations into conservative political attitudes.

The political attitudes were derived from an oblique factor analysis of more than 30 separate items covering diverse social and political stimuli. These items fell neatly into three separate scales, labeled general conservatism, racial conservatism, and moral conservatism. These three dependent variables were supplemented with the respondent's reported vote in the 1980 presidential election and stated partisan preference. [23] All five dependent variables were scored so they would vary positively with conservatism. (For information about all scales used in the analysis, see Appendix to Chapter 4.) The use of multiple dependent measures allowed us to determine if the impact of religion varied across sociopolitical domains, as some have suggested, or had a uniform impact.

These measures were entered into a series of multiple regression equations according to the principles of path analysis. On the basis of compelling evidence from other studies, we assumed religion would operate differently for blacks and whites, and thus we performed separate analyses for the two racial groups.[24] For both sets of respondents, variables were entered into the equation according to our assumptions about the tiers of causality. This means, for example, that "theocracy" was entered initially to explain the dependent measures, followed first by the set of three "religiosity" measures, then by the predisposing factors of localism and denominational background, and finally by the social background factors. Refer to Figure 4.1 for the assumptions about hierarchy that were followed in the regression equations.

RESULTS

The initial concern in our study was to reduce the list of predictors to a more manageable number, a task that was accomplished in two stages. The initial regression equations included all variables that we had reason to think would affect the dependent measures, either directly or through another variable. Variables were entered in steps (going backward in tiers from the dependent variable—see Figure 4.1) on the condition that their contribution to the dependent measure would be significant at the .01 level. Some variables that entered the equation early failed to retain the specified t-value after other variables (variables located at the beginning stages of the causal chain) were entered. These weakened predictors were dropped and the regression analyses were rerun.

After the first set of analyses, three variables—sex, parental socioeconomic status, and parental denomination—were removed for failing to achieve the specified significance level. The second stage revealed that three of the four religious measures lost significance by the time the final set of predictors had been entered. Church involvement, devotionalism, and theocracy all had t-values exceeding .01 when the equation was completed. These variables were thus removed when the final set of equations was calculated.

Results of the analyses for white respondents are displayed in Figure 4.2. The behavioral variable, reported presidential vote in 1980, was not related significantly to any of the predictors. Party

FIGURE 4.2

Path Coefficients for White Respondents

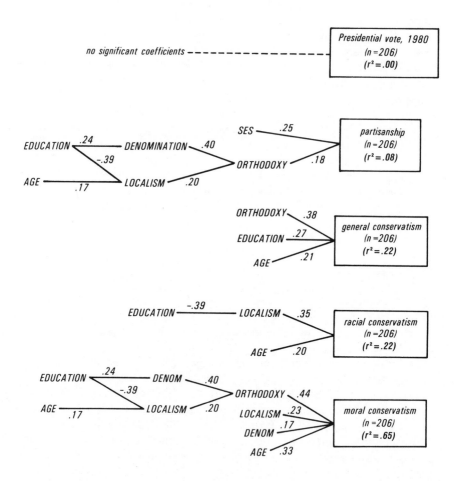

identification was significantly associated with respondent socioeconomic status (SES) and, weakly, with religious orthodoxy. Increases in SES were found to be associated with an increased propensity to identify with the Republican party, a finding that conforms to previous research on southern Republicanism.[25] The connection with orthodoxy supplies indirect links between partisanship and four of the antecedent variables: denomination, localism, education, and age.

The predictor variables proved considerably more powerful in explaining the attitudinal variables rather than the behavioral variables for white respondents. Racial conservatism was related to two of the social structural variables and the psychological orientation of localism. Localism and age each exerted direct positive effects on racial conservatism; age had an additional indirect influence through its association with localism, while education, a significant negative influence on localism, indirectly diminished racial conservatism. The pattern of causality was somewhat different for the measure of general conservatism, a scale composed of two economic and two noneconomic items. General conservatism varied directly as a function of religious orthodoxy, increased age, and increased education. It varied indirectly as a function of conservative denominational affiliation and increased localism, by virtue of the direct link between these two variables and orthodoxy. Taken together, the predictor variables explained between one-fifth and one-fourth of the total variation in the measures of racial and general conservatism.

The measure of moral conservatism proved to be very well explained by the various predictors. Orthodoxy, localism, denomination, and age each contributed directly and significantly to the level of commitment to traditional moral values. There were several indirect influences as well: denomination, localism, education, and age affected moral conservatism through their direct effects on other predictors. Taken together, these factors accounted for two-thirds of the variation in this dependent variable.

The analysis for black respondents, summarized in Figure 4.3, revealed few substantial relationships. Four of the dependent measures—reported presidential vote in 1980, party identification, racial conservatism, and general conservatism—were not significantly associated with a single predictor. For the first three of these factors, the explanation is simply a lack of statistical variance. Over 80 percent of the black respondents identified with the Democratic party, and all but a handful reported voting for Jimmy Carter or not going to the polls in 1980. Similarly, the blacks scored on the bottom of the racial conservatism scale, with individual results so tightly clustered about the mean that the variance, as measured by the coefficient of relative variation (standard deviation divided by the mean), was only 0.64. With such a high degree of within-group cohesion, none of the predictor variables could discriminate enough among individuals to attain significance. This explanation does not account for the inability to predict general conservatism, a variable on which black scores, though lower in the aggregate than white scores, were sufficiently dispersed to allow for significant associations with the predictors.

For blacks as well as whites, we had the greatest success in accounting for commitment to traditional moral values. There were substantial direct links between orthodoxy, localism, and age and the scale score on the moral conservatism index. In addition to these

FIGURE 4.3

Path Coefficients for Black Respondents

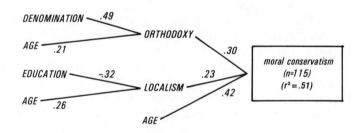

NO SIGNIFICANT COEFFICIENTS FOR:

Presidential vote, 1980
partisanship
general conservatism
racial conservatism

DENOMINATION —.49
AGE —.21
ORTHODOXY
.30
EDUCATION —-.32
.23
LOCALISM
.42
AGE —.26
AGE

moral conservatism
(n=115)
(r^2 = .51)

direct positive influences, the level of moral conservatism for blacks was indirectly affected by age (through localism and orthodoxy), by denomination (through orthodoxy), and negatively, by education (a negative influence on localism). The correlates of moral conservatism for blacks strongly resemble the pattern of causality discerned for white respondents. The predictors accounted for just over half the variance, making moral conservatism the best-predicted measure for respondents of both races.

CONCLUSION

The results of our study provide interesting insights for our principle conern, the independent role of religious belief in structuring political perceptions. For whites and blacks religious orthodoxy proved to be a significant direct influence on some of the dependent measures. In each case the relationship conformed to prediction, with orthodoxy contributing to the level of conservative political outlooks. These relationships proved robust enough to withstand the entry of several intervening factors (demographic characteristics, localism, and so forth), which other scholars have suggested as the real cause of the allegedly spurious links between religious and political conservatism. The impact of orthodoxy was doubly impressive because it was the only one of four religious measures to survive the stepwise analysis; its effect, as measured by the standardized regression coefficient, was larger than any other predictor for two of the scales for whites (moral conservatism and general conservatism), and it was the only scale that could be predicted for blacks. Of course, both of these outcomes may be due to the remarkably high degree of reliability of the othodoxy scale (alpha = .84), but the beta coefficients are impressive whatever the reason.[26]

Despite these positive findings, the results also point to important limitations on the political relevance of religious belief. First and foremost, it was noteworthy that orthodoxy did not help explain the level of racial conservatism among whites, was not the strongest predictor of general conservatism, and had no measurable impact on two key forms of behavior (party identification and 1980 presidential vote). As scholars, our ultimate concern is not to link attitudes to attitudes but to determine in what manner attitudes might ultimately affect political behavior. The absence of a link between orthodoxy and our two behavioral measures raises major questions about the political relevance of religious belief.

Essentially, the problem is to understand how voters do and do not translate their religious conservatism into conservative politics. In principle, partisanship and voting would seem to offer the orthodox fairly clear and unambiguous clues about appropriate behavior. In 1980 the Republican candidate for president, Ronald Reagan, espoused positions that were thought to have great appeal to the Evangelicals, and he received clear support from many of the most prominent figures of the religious Right. The rise of Republicanism in west Tennessee has also been based on issues that would seem to have great attraction for the orthodox. Yet, despite the apparent affinity, there were no observed links between orthodoxy and either presidential vote or political partisanship.

Perhaps orthodoxy can influence political behavior only in the absence of countervailing factors. Clearly, for black voters the imperative of race overshadows all other considerations. As a minority group whose political perspectives are shaped by out-group status, blacks achieve remarkably high levels of political cohesion with little evidence of internal cleavages based on other social characteristics. As long as blacks pursue a politics of group interest, it is unlikely that religious factors will contribute to partisan differentiation within the black community.

For whites, the absence of an orthodoxy effect on behavior may be due to several factors. Despite the rise of Republicanism, the Democratic party still enjoys substantial support among older whites who have not been able to shake a traditional attachment to the party of the Confederacy. These traditional Democrats—older, less educated, generally of lower socioeconomic status—come from the very milieu that promotes religious Fundamentalism. The Republican resurgence is most likely fueled by economic groups for whom the process of upward social mobility has diminished the hold of Fundamentalist religion. In addition to the persistence of a Democratic tradition among many of the orthodox, there was in 1980 the additional factor of Jimmy Carter's own religious Fundamentalism. National poll data indicate that Carter appears to have fared rather better among southern white Protestants than recent Democratic candidates, a tendency that has been attributed to his personal piety. [27] The pull of voting for a fellow Baptist may have outweighed the conservatism of the Republican candidate for a substantial share of the electorate in 1980. Together, the persistence of attachment to the Democrats and Carter's affinity with the Fundamentalist tradition may help to account for the absence of behavioral uniformity among the orthodox.

Beyond these factors we must consider the implications of our results for the continuing effort to mobilize orthodox voters on behalf of conservative causes. Orthodoxy proved most powerful in explaining what has been termed moral conservatism. The items on this scale involve many of the so-called family issues—abortion, women's rights, sexuality, drugs, and so forth—where the link between religious precepts and politics is perhaps the most obvious. Orthodox

voters seem to have more difficulty perceiving the religious dimension
in issues such as balancing the budget and race relations, and thus
they are less likely to translate their religious conservatism into
political terms. This seems to present a dilemma to those who seek
to harness the Evangelicals as part of a new conservative majority.
In order to attract support from the orthodox, conservatives need to
stress issues such as abortion, sexuality, and women's rights. Yet
these issues do not seem to appeal to many voters who might otherwise favor a conservative candidate on economic grounds.[28] If the
new Right puts its major emphasis on economic goals, it loses its
special appeal for the orthodox, who—Jerry Falwell to the contrary—
apparently do not see a balanced budget as a moral issue, at least not
to the same degree as they are attracted to abortion or state-sanctioned
homosexuality as issues. But if the emphasis is on the social issues
that have such strong appeal to the orthodox, the Right will probably
be limited in its support to a clear minority of the electorate.

This analysis thus suggests that the impact of religious belief
depends upon the nature of the issue and the political context. Despite
these limitations, the results do confirm Ann Hohmann's conjecture
that more fully specified research designs will enable us to detect
subtle yet important variations in secular political behavior attributable
to the influence of the religious factor.[29]

APPENDIX TO CHAPTER 4

Derivation of Measures

Orthodoxy
(alpha = .84)

1. To me, the things of this world are not very important; what
   really matters is what happens after death.
2. We need to bring America back to Christian values.
3. Jesus is the divine son of God and I have no doubts about it.
4. I know God really exists and I have no doubts about it.
5. Part of being a good Christian may involve helping other people
   but it is more important to develop a close relationship with God.
6. Miracles actually happened just as the Bible says.
7. The devil actually exists.
8. If enough people were brought to Christ, most social ills would
   take care of themselves.
9. Living by God's principles makes a nation great.
10. Do you consider yourself to be a born-again Christian?
11. Have you ever had the feeling that you were somehow in the
    presence of God?

12. Have you ever felt a sense of being saved in Christ?
13. It should be against the law to do anything that the Bible says is wrong.
14. If a person wants to go to heaven, how important is it to believe in Jesus Christ as savior?

Theocracy
(alpha = .61)

1. Christians should get more involved in politics.
2. During the last elections, Christian groups were very active in a lot of campaigns. What do you think of that?

Church Activity
(alpha = .83)

1. In an average year, how often do you attend worship services?
2. Do you belong to any church organizations or get involved in any church activities besides worship?

Devotionalism
(alpha = .66)

1. Do you regularly listen to any church services on radio or watch them on television?
2. Do you ever pray privately, when you're not at church?
3. Where you live now, do you regularly say table prayers or grace in your home?

Localism
(alpha = .63)

1. Despite all the news about national and international events, what goes on right here in Memphis is more interesting.
2. When it comes time to vote for candidates in local elections, I prefer a person whose family is known and well established.

Moral Conservatism
(alpha = .84)

1. The government in Memphis should be allowed to ban books and movies that it thinks are harmful to the public.
2. It should be against the law to do anything that the Bible says is wrong.
3. Department stores should be closed on Sunday.
4. The government should prohibit the private use of marijuana.
5. There should be laws against marriage between blacks and whites.

6. The schools are the wrong place to teach children about sex.
7. Women are happiest if they stick to keeping a house and raising children.
8. Abortion should be a private matter between a woman and her doctor.
9. Homosexuals should be able to do what they want to so long as they don't hurt other people.
10. If a man and woman want to live together without getting married, that's their business.
11. Birth control devices should be available to any adult who wants them.

General Conservatism
(alpha = . 63)

1. We must balance the federal budget even if it means cutting back on programs like social security and veterans' benefits.
2. The police in Memphis are too quick to use force when they arrest a suspect.
3. Generally speaking, we don't spend enough on welfare programs in this country.
4. Students in public schools should have the right to voluntary prayers and Bible reading.
5. The government should guarantee every citizen a minimum standard of living.

Racial Conservatism
(alpha = . 64)

1. White people have a right to keep blacks out of their neighborhood if they want to.
2. America is a better country because racial discrimination has been made illegal.
3. There should be laws against marriage between blacks and whites.
4. The churches should do a lot more to reduce prejudice and discrimination.
5. America will be a better country if our schools are integrated.

NOTES

1. Leon D. Epstein, Political Parties in Western Democracies (New York: Praeger, 1967), p. 88.
2. Compare Philip E. Converse, "Some Priority Variables in Comparative Research," in Electoral Behavior: A Comparative Handbook, ed. Richard Rose (New York: Free Press, 1974), pp. 733-35.

3. See Benton Johnson and Richard H. White, "Protestantism, Political Preference and the Nature of Religious Influence: Comment on Anderson's Paper," Review of Religious Research 9 (Fall 1967): 31-32.

4. John M. Hammond, "Revival Religion and Antislavery Politics," American Sociological Review 39 (April 1974): 175-86.

5. Compare Michael Parenti, "Political Values and Religious Cultures: Jews, Catholics and Protestants," Journal for the Scientific Study of Religion 6 (Fall 1967): 259-69; Richard J. Stellway, "The Correspondence between Religious Orientation and Socio-Political Liberalism and Conservatism," Sociological Quarterly 14 (Summer 1973): 430-39; Leo Driedger, "Doctrinal Belief: A Major Factor in the Differential Perception of Social Issues," Sociological Quarterly 15 (Winter 1974): 66-80; John M. Hammond, The Politics of Benevolence: Revival Religion and American Voting Behavior (Norwood, N.J.: Ablex, 1979); and Kenneth D. Wald, Crosses on the Ballot: Patterns of British Voter Alignment since 1885 (Princeton, N.J.: Princeton University Press, 1983).

6. Dean Rojek, "The Protestant Ethic and Political Preference," Social Forces 52 (December 1973): 168-77; Robert Wuthnow, "Religious Commitment and Conservatism: In Search of an Elusive Relationship," in Religion in Sociological Perspective, ed. Charles Y. Glock (Belmont, Calif.: Wadsworth, 1973), pp. 117-32; and Carol Mueller, "In Search of a Constituency for the 'New Right'" (Paper presented at the 1981 Annual Meeting of the American Political Science Association, New York, September 3-6, 1981).

7. Wuthnow, "Religious Commitment and Conservatism."

8. When fieldwork began, the 1980 census data had not yet been released, so we had to rely on the 1970 data. Midway through the project, the racial composition of the Standard Metropolitan Statistical Area according to the 1980 census became available, and we adjusted the quotas to reflect the increase in the black proportion of the population.

9. The initial interviewing was conducted by students in our jointly taught course on political psychology. At the conclusion of the semester we decided to expand the sample to approximately 400, and the quotas were revised upward. The additional interviews were the responsibility of upper-division and graduate students in psychology courses.

10. At approximately the same time we were in the field, Larry Petersen of the Department of Sociology at Memphis State University was conducting a telephone survey on religion and various social attitudes. Using systematic random sampling from the Memphis telephone directory, Petersen obtained a sample (N = 334) very similar to ours, especially in terms of religious affiliation. The strong similarity of

our sample to that obtained by Petersen confirms our belief that quota sampling did not bias the sample in any important respect.

11. Compare Peter J. Henriot, "The Coincidence of Political and Religious Attitudes," Review of Religious Research 8 (Fall 1966): 50-58; and Richard Quinney, "Political Conservatism, Alienation and Fatalism: Contingencies of Social Status and Religious Fundamentalism," Sociometry 27 (September 1964): 372-81.

12. Robert Lane, Political Life (New York: Free Press, 1959).

13. Albert J. Reiss, Occupations and Social Status (New York: Free Press, 1961), pp. 263-75.

14. Parental SES was the average of the socioeconomic index scores of both parents; if only one parent reported an occupation, that score was assigned as the parental SES. A similar rule was followed in assigning respondent status: the score was the mean value for respondent and spouse, the value of respondent's occupation if he or she was unmarried or the only employed member of the household. Students were assigned the parental status scores.

15. Fred W. Grupp and William M. Newman, "Political Ideology and Religious Preference: The John Birch Society and Americans for Democratic Action," Journal for the Scientific Study of Religion 12 (December 1973): 401-13. The Grupp and Newman classification was revised in several minor respects to reflect more accurately the pattern of orthodoxy in the South. We added predominantly black Methodists (such as African Methodist Episcopal) to the category of conservative Protestants, and members of the Christian Church and the United Church of Christ were added to the moderate camp. Southern Baptists, whom Grupp and Newman had included with Fundamentalists, were treated as a separate group. Because the Catholics in our sample had a lower mean score on orthodoxy than the conservative Protestants, we reversed their order in the Grupp and Newman classification and assigned the latter a higher scale score.

16. Wade Clark Roof, "Religious Orthodoxy and Minority Prejudice: Causal Relationships or Reflection of Localistic World View?" American Journal of Sociology 80 (November 1974): 643-64.

17. Rodney Stark and Charles Y. Glock, American Piety: The Nature of Religious Commitment (Berkeley and Los Angeles: University of California Press, 1970).

18. See John Wilson, Religion in American Society: The Effective Presence (Englewood Cliffs, N.J.: Prentice-Hall, 1978), pp. 447-48.

19. Harold E. Quinley, "The Dilemma of an Activist Church: Protestant Religion in the Sixties and Seventies," Journal for the Scientific Study of Religion 13 (March 1974): 1-22.

20. Charles H. Anderson, "Religious Communality and Party Preference," Sociological Analysis 30 (Spring 1969): 32-41; and Johnson and White, "Comment on Anderson's Paper."

21. Virginia Gray, "Antievolution Sentiment and Behavior: The Case of Arkansas," Journal of American History 57 (September 1970): 352-66; and Quinney, "Social Status and Religious Fundamentalism."

22. In view of the active involvement of conservative religious groups in 1980, this scale probably measures reaction to groups such as the Moral Majority rather than to the general issue of religious group activity in campaigns. This does not hold for black respondents, who appear to have perceived the question in the context of active mobilization by the predominantly black churches on behalf of President Jimmy Carter.

23. Party identification was determined by following up the standard Center for Political Studies question with a probe for Independents only, asking if the respondent generally found himself or herself closer to one of the parties. Persons who refused to admit to a preference on both questions were classified as Independents, and all others were classified as affiliates of the party that was named. This tripartite division proved a better predictor of voting than a more complicated five-part scale, which assigned persons who admitted partisanship on the follow-up to an intermediate "weak partisan" scale.

24. See, for example, H. Irvin Penfield and Natalie M. Davis, "The Religious Right: A Southern Phenomenon" (Paper presented at the 1981 Annual Meeting of the Southern Political Science Association, Memphis, Tenn., November 5-7, 1981).

25. Louis M. Seagull, Southern Republicanism (Cambridge, Mass.: Schenkman, 1975).

26. Additional analysis using LISREL (a statistical technique that corrects for attenuation due to unreliability of composite measures) might clarify whether the superior power of orthodoxy over the other religious scales is genuine. See Russell J. Dalton, "Reassessing Parental Socialization: Indicator Unreliability versus Generational Transfer," American Political Science Review 74 (June 1980): 421-31.

27. Seymour Martin Lipset and Earl Rabb, "The Election and the Evangelicals," Commentary 71 (March 1981): 25-31, especially p. 27.

28. George Gallup, Jr., "Divining the Devout: The Polls and Religious Belief," Public Opinion 4 (April-May 1981): 41.

29. Ann A. Hohmann, "Political Conservatism and Fundamentalist Christianity: A Reexamination" (Paper presented at the 1980 Annual Meeting of the Midwest Political Science Association, Chicago, April 23-26, 1980).

PART II

SOUTHERN POLITICS AND RELIGION: ELITE PERSPECTIVES

INTRODUCTION TO PART II

While the chapters in Part I deal with religion and southern politics at the mass level, those in Part II focus on religion and southern politics at the elite level. Just as the mass citizenry is politically important in numerous ways—in constraining governmental action, for example—elites are important in helping to define the political agenda and in establishing and implementing public policy. [1] The study of elites of various types, therefore, has long occupied a prominent position in political research. [2] This is true as well for research on southern politics. [3]

The following chapters examine data on two types of elites, state party activists and Southern Baptist ministers. In Chapter 5 Robert P. Steed, Laurence W. Moreland, and Tod A. Baker utilize data generated by a survey of delegates to the 1980 state party conventions in seven states to examine the political impact of Fundamentalists in the South. These authors make a series of comparisons of white Fundamentalists across regional lines (South versus non-South) and of white Fundamentalists and non-Fundamentalists within the two broadly defined regions. The groups are compared in terms of socioeconomic, demographic, and political backgrounds; general political philosophy and specific issue positions; and candidate orientations.

In Chapter 6 Tod A. Baker, Robert P. Steed, and Laurence W. Moreland examine data from the same convention delegate survey but concentrate on an analysis of issue positions within the two southern states included in the study, South Carolina and Virginia. They employ discriminant analysis to explore the relative importance of race, partisan affiliation, and religion (Fundamentalism) in differentiating these southern delegates in terms of various issue dimensions. Then the implications of these data are considered for the question of continued southern distinctiveness.

In Chapter 7 Alan Abramowitz, John McGlennon, and Ronald Rapoport examine the role of Fundamentalists in recent Virginia politics. They review the involvement of "born-agains" in the 1978 Democratic senatorial nominating convention and the subsequent election campaign, and then they examine data on Fundamentalist involvement in the state's 1980 presidential nominating conventions with special attention to Fundamentalism in the Republican convention.

Finally, in Chapter 8 James Guth shifts the focus away from state party elites to a group of religious elites. He analyzes data from a survey of Southern Baptist ministers in an effort to ascertain their views toward organizations such as the Moral Majority, their personal political predispositions, their orientations toward political activism, and their own levels of political activity. Guth approaches the linkage between religion and politics in the South from the perspective of a religious elite that occupies a central place in southern culture and society.

Together these chapters provide a range of material that usefully complements the discussions on religion and southern politics at the mass level in Part I of this book.

NOTES

1. On the role of elites in a democratic political system, see, among others, Dennis S. Ippolito, Thomas G. Walker, and Kenneth L. Kolson, Public Opinion and Responsible Democracy (Englewood Cliffs, N.J.: Prentice-Hall, 1976). An excellent statement on the roles of party leaders may be found in Samuel J. Eldersveld, Political Parties: A Behavioral Analysis (Chicago: Rand McNally, 1964), especially chap. 1.

2. The extensive array of literature on governmental and organizational leaders and activists of all types attests to the importance of elite research in political science (and in related social sciences). Over two decades ago, a partial bibliography on political leadership contained over 600 entries, and there is no evidence that interest (and, consequently, research) has diminished. See Wendell Bell, Richard J. Hill, and Charles R. Wright, Public Leadership (San Francisco: Chandler, 1961).

3. For some indications of the range of research on southern elites, see, for example, Lester M. Salamon, "Leadership and Mobilization: The Emerging Black Political Elite in the American South," Journal of Politics 35 (August 1973): 615-46; Earl Black, Southern Governors and Civil Rights (Cambridge, Mass.: Harvard University Press, 1976); and Robert P. Steed, Tod A. Baker, and Laurence W. Moreland, "In-Migration and Southern State Party Elites" (Paper presented at the 1981 Annual Meeting of the Southern Political Science Association, Atlanta, November 5-7, 1981).

5

RELIGION AND PARTY ACTIVISTS: FUNDAMENTALISM AND POLITICS IN REGIONAL PERSPECTIVE

Robert P. Steed
Laurence W. Moreland
Tod A. Baker

INTRODUCTION

The emergence of Fundamentalist religious organizations as a supposedly powerful political force was one of the most highly publicized features of the 1980 elections.[1] The popular press and many candidates maintained that groups such as Moral Majority and Christian Viewpoint were important, and sometimes even decisive, in influencing the policy positions of candidates and political parties and in affecting the outcomes of specific elections.[2] These claims were understandably encouraged, supported, and probably embellished by the Fundamentalist organizations themselves as their leaders and members basked in the spotlight of their newfound national political clout.[3] Although the accuracy of such claims may be in doubt (a point explored by various other chapters in this volume), there is little doubt that the political efforts of these organized Fundamentalist groups were matters of considerable concern and importance for political parties, candidates, and other political groups involved in the 1980 elections.[4]

Although the level of interest in connections between religious Fundamentalism and politics, especially by the press and the general public, has been abnormally high during the period since the early stages of the 1980 election campaigns, the broader topic has long fascinated social scientists in a variety of disciplines. Within a large body of literature concerning the more general relationship between religion and politics a number of studies have focused on identifying

We gratefully acknowledge the financial support for this research provided by The Citadel Development Foundation.

and mapping linkages between Fundamentalism and specific political attitudes and behaviors. With few exceptions, most of the research in this area has depicted Fundamentalists as more politically conservative on a series of issues than non-Fundamentalists.[5] For example, several studies have found Fundamentalism to be related to support for prohibition, antigambling, and Sunday-closing laws.[6] Similarly, Fundamentalists have been found to be more opposed to abortion, homosexuality, and legalization of marijuana than non-Fundamentalists.[7] While the data are not as clear in other areas, there is also some evidence that Fundamentalism tends to be positively related to economic conservatism and anti-Semitism and negatively related to tolerance of people with different opinions and life-styles (for example, homosexuals, communists, and atheists) and to support for the civil rights movement.[8] Finally, Fundamentalists have been found traditionally to be relatively uninvolved in politics and related social movements. Although there have been some notable exceptions,[9] the Fundamentalist approach to society has been more evangelistic than political and more otherworldly than this-worldly except in selected cases involving perceived individual morality (for example, prohibition, gambling, and sexual permissiveness).[10]

For students of southern politics, interest in the connections between religious Fundamentalism and politics long predates the 1980 elections. Historically, the strongly Fundamentalist nature of southern religion has been considered a key element in setting the region apart from the remainder of the nation. For example, writing in the mid-1960s Samuel Hill identified a number of key differences between the South and non-South in terms of religion and he noted that the South, with its remarkable transdenominational homogeneity dominated by Southern Baptists and Methodists, remains a clearly distinct region religiously.[11] The predominance of Protestant Fundamentalism in the South has been noticed as a distinguishing feature by other scholars as well, including the sociologist John Shelton Reed and the geographers James R. Shortridge and Wilbur Zelinsky.[12] In fact, in Shortridge's view the South is one of the most clearly defined religious regions in the country, and he argued convincingly that "a religious regionalization is as close to an objective general cultural regionalization as we are likely to get in the foreseeable future."[13]

However, an important consideration is whether, beyond its greater proportions in the South than in the non-South, Fundamentalism in the region is demonstrably different politically from Fundamentalism outside the region. Fundamentalism may have different influences on southern and nonsouthern politics mainly (or only) because it is more widespread and pervasive in the South; on the other hand, southern Fundamentalism and nonsouthern Fundamentalism may differ in their respective relationships with regional politics qualitatively as well as

quantitatively. In either case comparative evidence should help to un-
ravel the complex connections between southern Fundamentalism and
southern politics.

A number of studies have strongly suggested that Fundamenta-
ism in the South has a different impact on politics than Fundamentalism outside the region. For example, an analysis of National Opinion
Research Center (NORC) data for the period 1972-78 by Ted Jelen indicated that southern Fundamentalists tend to be less tolerant of communists, homosexuals, and atheists than nonsouthern Fundamentalists.[14] A somewhat broader discussion presented in the early 1960s
by W. Seward Salisbury focused on dividing northern and southern
samples of college students into orthodox and unorthodox religious
groups and comparing them along several dimensions.[15] While he
did not specifically study Fundamentalism, his characterization of
those classified as orthodox closely parallels the usual description
of Fundamentalists. It is therefore useful in indicating some relevant
regional differences. Salisbury noted that Southerners classified as
orthodox tend to be considerably more opposed to interracial marriage,
much more desirous of and supportive of segregated schools, significantly less willing to extend full pastoral rights to women, and much
more likely to find some good resulting from war than their orthodox
brethren outside the South. Interestingly, these regional differences
existed within a context of sharp orthodox-unorthodox variations that
transcended region. In other words, orthodox students tend to be
sharply more conservative than unorthodox students on these types
of issues regardless of their regions of residence, but among orthodox students clear regional differences are evident.[16]

In this vein, most significantly, a sizable body of research has
documented the distinctive positions taken by southern Fundamentalist churches (clergy and congregation) on the question of racial integration in the 1950s and 1960s at the height of the civil rights movement. For the most part the record was, at best, one of a mildly
conservative posture of keeping the church out of the battle in the name
of otherworldly evangelism in preference to this-worldly social reform; at worst, it was a staunchly conservative defense of the segregated status quo under the supposed biblical injunction to maintain
racial purity.[17] In any event there was little doubt that southern Fundamentalists stood apart from their nonsouthern counterparts on this
issue.

Beyond its greater prevalence, then, there is evidence that
southern Fundamentalism has differed from nonsouthern Fundamentalism in its impact on regional politics. Such analyses leave at least
three main questions unanswered, however. First, do such variations
between southern and nonsouthern Fundamentalists at the mass level
continue through the 1980 elections? To some extent, the earlier

chapters of this volume have addressed that point and, consequently, it is not our concern here. Second, do regional differences between Fundamentalists extend beyond the level of the electorate to apply as well to political activists? The material reviewed above is based on studies of the mass public and therefore reveals relatively little about the comparative importance of religious Fundamentalism for political activists. Since activists tend to differ from the general public in certain basic attitudinal and behavioral respects, it is by no means certain that conclusions concerning Fundamentalism and politics within the electorate apply equally usefully to political activists. [18] Given the importance of political activists in helping to shape and implement public policy and political agendas, it is worthwhile to explore this dimension of Fundamentalism in contemporary southern politics. Finally, are any or all of the interregional differences between Fundamentalists reflected in differences in their respective impacts on the regional political systems within which they operate? Most previous research has focused on interregional differences between southern and nonsouthern Fundamentalists. While such an approach is useful, it does not directly compare intraregional patterns of Fundamentalist impact on politics. Comparing the political influence of Fundamentalism within the respective regions would provide an additional dimension to the attempt to understand linkages between religion and southern politics.

This chapter addresses the last two points by presenting comparative data on Fundamentalism and a series of selected personal and political variables drawn from a study of delegates to the 1980 Democratic and Republican state conventions in seven states. Insofar as two of these states are in the South and five are outside the South, this provides information on the nature and importance of Fundamentalism for southern and nonsouthern party activists within the context of the 1980 elections. The analysis will deal only with white delegates because there is substantial evidence that Fundamentalism among blacks is significantly different in its political consequences than Fundamentalism among whites (and it is the latter that has attracted most recent attention and created most of the current excitement). [19] In addition, since most past research on religious Fundamentalism and its connections to southern politics has been concerned with white Fundamentalists (at least partially in recognition of the region's political dominance by whites, historically), there is further logic in restricting the racial focus in this analysis. Discussion follows two broad lines: it compares Fundamentalists in the South and non-South on selected variables, and it considers the relative patterns of Fundamentalist/non-Fundamentalist differences within each region.

METHODOLOGY

The data for this study come from an extensive questionnaire administered to delegates to the 1980 state conventions held in seven of the thirteen states that utilized, at least in part, the caucus-convention system of selecting delegates to their 1980 presidential nominating conventions. Two states, Virginia and South Carolina, are southern; the other five, Arizona, Colorado, Maine, Iowa, and North Dakota, are nonsouthern. One item on the questionnaire asked respondents if they considered themselves to be religious Fundamentalists. That question provides the basic categories for comparison in this chapter. Approximately 12,400 delegates completed questionnaires, with response rates in the various states ranging from 25 to 75 percent.

PERSONAL BACKGROUNDS OF ACTIVISTS

If southern and nonsouthern Fundamentalists among the state party activists examined here differ politically, it is apparently not a result of significant variations in their personal backgrounds. At least there are almost no differences between these groups on the standard background variables included in this study (see Table 5.1). Differences on age, sex, and residential patterns are so small as to to virtually inconsequential. In both regions Fundamentalists tend to be middle-aged, slightly more representative of males than of females, predominantly from rural/small-town areas, and relatively long-term residents of their current home states. Also, in each region the Fundamentalist delegates differ from the non-Fundamentalist delegates in the same general ways (to the extent that they differ at all).

With regard to education and income, southern and nonsouthern Fundamentalists differ a little more clearly, with southern Fundamentalists being slightly better educated and somewhat more affluent in the aggregate than their nonsouthern counterparts, but even on these variables the differences are not significant. For example, only 8 percent more of the southern Fundamentalists than the nonsouthern Fundamentalists have at least a college education (48 percent versus 40 percent); an identical 8 percent difference exists between the two groups with respect to annual income of $35,000 or more (30 percent versus 22 percent). Finally, in comparison with non-Fundamentalists in each region, Fundamentalists tend to be similarly less educated and less wealthy.

In terms of denominational affiliations, both groups of Fundamentalists are similar in that they are both overwhelmingly Protestant.

TABLE 5.1

Personal Background Characteristics of State Party Activists, Controlling for Region and Fundamentalism
(in percent)

	Southern		Nonsouthern	
	Fundamentalist	Non-Fundamentalist	Fundamentalist	Non-Fundamentalist
Age				
18–34	28	30	25	33
35–54	47	44	45	44
55 and over	25	26	30	23
Total	100	100	100	100
(N)	(1,174)	(2,525)	(1,309)	(5,188)
Sex				
Female	44	46	46	46
Male	56	54	54	54
Total	100	100	100	100
(N)	(1,185)	(2,543)	(1,317)	(5,200)
Education				
Some high school or less	5	2	6	3
High school graduate	15	7	20	12
Some college	31	24	33	27
College graduate	21	25	18	25
Postcollege education	27	42	22	33
Total	99	100	99	100
(N)	(1,181)	(2,541)	(1,314)	(5,203)
Income				
$0–$14,999	17	8	21	17
$15,000–$24,999	29	20	33	29

$25,000–$34,999	24	25	23	24
$35,000–$44,999	14	19	10	14
$45,000–$59,999	8	14	6	7
$60,000 and over	8	14	6	8
Total	100	100	99	99
(N)	(1,088)	(2,422)	(1,256)	(5,026)
Type of residence				
Urban/suburban	24	43	20	23
Rural/small town	74	54	79	76
Other	1	2	1	1
Total	99	99	100	100
(N)	(1,164)	(2,513)	(1,312)	(5,182)
Length of residence in present home state				
Less than 5 years	8	8	7	7
5–10 years	10	13	9	11
10–20 years	19	22	14	15
Over 20 years	63	57	70	66
Total	100	100	100	99
(N)	(1,173)	(2,534)	(1,318)	(5,196)
Denominational affiliations				
Baptist	52	9	22	2
Methodist	14	18	13	12
Presbyterian	11	13	6	6
Lutheran	2	5	17	13
Episcopal	6	18	3	6
Other Protestant	10	12	27	21
Catholic	4	15	11	27
Jewish	0	3	0	2
None	1	7	1	11
Total	100	100	100	100
(N)	(1,173)	(2,448)	(1,287)	(4,948)

111

However, within this broad context are some variations. A majority of southern Fundamentalists are Baptists, with Methodists and Presbyterians ranking a distant second and third, respectively. Taken together, these three denominations account for over three-fourths (77 percent) of the southern Fundamentalists. In contrast, these denominations account for less than half (41 percent) of the nonsouthern Fundamentalists, with the bulk of the differential resulting from the significantly lower proportion of Baptists among these activists. Similarly, Lutherans constitute a greater percentage and Presbyterians a clearly lower percentage of the nonsouthern Fundamentalists. There are also some modest differences in the percentages of Catholics in each group of Fundamentalists. In general, both southern and nonsouthern Fundamentalists are basically Protestant, but the latter aggregate is spread much more among a number of denominations whereas southern Fundamentalists are considerably more concentrated, especially within the cluster of Baptist churches in the region. This is not particularly surprising because it is generally consistent with the reports of Baptist-Methodist prevalence within the southern population noted earlier. Whether the overarching Protestantism of southern and nonsouthern Fundamentalist activists is more or less important as a political variable than the doctrinal variations associated with different patterns of denominational affiliation within that Protestantism is a question lying beyond the scope of this chapter, but it is the one background variable examined here that is at least mildly suggestive in its implications for helping to explain regional political variations among Fundamentalists.

Within each region, Fundamentalist activists are similarly more Baptist and less Episcopalian, Catholic, and Jewish than non-Fundamentalist activists. The two groups tend to have broadly similar proportions of Methodists and Presbyterians, with Lutheran attachments showing a mixed pattern.

While there is little in the background data to lead us to expect political differences between southern and nonsouthern Fundamentalists, nevertheless political attitudes and behavior are often influenced by factors other than personal characteristics. Because southern politics has historically differed from the politics of other parts of the nation, it may be that the political backgrounds of these party activists exhibit patterns sufficiently different to suggest (and help account for) variations in their political orientations.

POLITICAL BACKGROUNDS OF ACTIVISTS

In contrast to the general similarity of their personal backgrounds, southern and nonsouthern Fundamentalists differ rather clearly on two of the key political background variables in Table 5.2. First, their patterns of party identification vary. Southern Fundamentalists are much more Republican than nonsouthern Fundamentalists. Although both groups tend to be more Republican than Democratic, the nonsouthern Fundamentalists split almost in half on this point while over two-thirds of the southern Fundamentalists are Republicans.

Second, the levels of past campaign activity for each group vary. Southern Fundamentalists exhibit greater levels of activity than nonsouthern Fundamentalists, a point possibly suggesting that southern Fundamentalism is more intimately connected to regional politics than is nonsouthern Fundamentalism. However, while southern Fundamentalists are more active, they do not indicate a longer history of party activity than their nonsouthern brethren. In fact, for these delegates exactly the same proportions of southern and nonsouthern Fundamentalists attended their first party convention beyond the local level in 1980. Similarly, there are almost no differences whatsoever between these groups with respect to length of party activity in their present states. Interestingly, the figures indicate that Fundamentalists in both regions are relative newcomers to the political arena. This point seems to be consistent with those analyses of the 1980 elections arguing that the surge of Fundamentalist involvement in politics is a fairly recent development; however, the data showing almost identical figures for non-Fundamentalists in each region moderate this conclusion considerably by indicating that all these delegates, regardless of their religious predispositions, are almost equally new political activists.

Finally, a comparison of delegates' motivations for becoming involved in the 1980 presidential campaign shows very little variation between southern and nonsouthern Fundamentalists (see Table 5.3). For both groups the most important motivations are to work for strongly favored issues, to support a particular candidate, to support the political party, and to meet civic responsibility; to develop a political career and to enjoy the visibility of being a candidate are reported to be the least important motivations for each aggregate. Moreover, in each region comparisons of Fundamentalists and non-Fundamentalists show a similar lack of variation in motivations. In brief, there is little to suggest significantly diverse motivational patterns for the groups under examination.

In summary, the key political background differences between southern and nonsouthern Fundamentalists concern party affiliation and level of party activity. Of these, party identification patterns might be expected to be of some importance in contributing to different political orientations for southern and nonsouthern Fundamental-

TABLE 5.2

Political Background Characteristics of State Party Activists, Controlling for Region and Fundamentalism
(in percent)

	Southern		Nonsouthern	
	Fundamentalist	Non-Fundamentalist	Fundamentalist	Non-Fundamentalist
Party affiliation				
Democratic	30	46	48	63
Republican	70	54	52	37
Total	100	100	100	100
(N)	(1,186)	(2,548)	(1,319)	(5,211)
Length of party activity in present home state (years)				
Less than 5	42	40	41	40
5–10	20	25	19	22
10–20	20	22	20	21
Over 20	18	13	20	17
Total	100	100	100	100
(N)	(1,177)	(2,532)	(1,312)	(5,181)
Delegate to any other past state or national convention?				
Yes	50	58	50	53
No	50	42	50	47
Total	100	100	100	100
(N)	(1,178)	(2,532)	(1,133)	(4,488)
Level of past campaign activity				
Active in all	36	44	25	26
Active in most	25	26	23	25
Active in a few	25	22	33	32
Active in none	14	8	19	17
Total	100	100	100	100
(N)	(1,166)	(2,530)	(1,287)	(5,136)

Source: Compiled by the authors from state party convention data.

114

TABLE 5.3

Motivations of State Party Activists, Controlling for Region and Fundamentalism
(in percent)

Motivation	Southern		Nonsouthern	
	Fundamentalist	Non-Fundamentalist	Fundamentalist	Non-Fundamentalist
To support the party				
Important	94	93	92	88
Not important	6	7	8	12
Total	100	100	100	100
(N)	(1,146)	(2,469)	(1,263)	(4,983)
To help my own political career				
Important	22	21	17	17
Not important	78	79	83	83
Total	100	100	100	100
(N)	(1,023)	(2,272)	(1,151)	(4,690)
Campaign excitement				
Important	47	53	53	55
Not important	53	47	47	45
Total	100	100	100	100
(N)	(1,041)	(2,322)	(1,177)	(4,770)
To meet other people				
Important	70	68	71	69
Not important	30	32	29	31
Total	100	100	100	100
(N)	(1,059)	(2,332)	(1,176)	(4,759)
				(continued)

TABLE 5.3 (continued)

Motivation	Southern		Nonsouthern	
	Fundamentalist	Non-Fundamentalist	Fundamentalist	Non-Fundamentalist
To support a particular candidate				
Important	96	94	94	92
Not important	4	6	6	8
Total	100	100	100	100
(N)	(1,140)	(2,431)	(1,234)	(4,890)
To work for strongly favored issues				
Important	98	96	97	95
Not important	2	4	3	5
Total	100	100	100	100
(N)	(1,125)	(2,442)	(1,249)	(4,926)
To enjoy the visibility of being a candidate				
Important	32	25	32	27
Not important	68	75	68	73
Total	100	100	100	100
(N)	(1,057)	(2,325)	(1,172)	(4,736)
Civic responsibility				
Important	91	87	89	84
Not important	9	13	11	16
Total	100	100	100	100
(N)	(1,118)	(2,431)	(1,242)	(4,940)

Source: Compiled by the authors from state party convention delegate data.

116

ists, although the relationship might well run in the opposite direction with different party identification patterns simply reflecting any regional differences between the Fundamentalist delegates' political positions. In any event, a central point is whether such political differences between the two groups exist at all, and if they do, whether these differences are reflected in variations in intraregional patterns of Fundamentalist political impact.

IDEOLOGICAL AND ISSUE POSITIONS OF ACTIVISTS

In the most general sense, our initial comparison of political attitudes reveals that southern Fundamentalists differ sharply from nonsouthern Fundamentalists with regard to their subjective political philosophy (see Table 5.4). Fundamentalist delegates from the South evince a great deal more conservatism than their counterparts from outside the region. Whereas a majority of each group is conservative (and in each case clearly more so than the non-Fundamentalists in the respective regions), a significantly greater proportion of the southern Fundamentalists indicate being either somewhat conservative or very conservative (77 percent versus 58 percent of the nonsouthern Fundamentalists). Similarly, the percentage of nonsouthern Fundamentalists indicating that they are at least somewhat liberal more than doubles the comparable percentage of southern Fundamentalists (25 percent versus 10 percent).

Moving from general political ideology to positions on a series of specific issues that were important during the 1980 campaign period, the greater conservatism of the southern Fundamentalists as compared with nonsouthern Fundamentalists is consistently translated into greater conservatism on particular policy questions (see Table 5.5). With only one exception where the differences are so small as to be inconsequential (imposition of mandatory wage and price controls to deal with inflation), southern Fundamentalists are proportionately more conservative on each of the 13 issues examined. While some of the differences are relatively minor, others are quite substantial. The largest variations occur on items concerning increased U.S. military presence in the Middle East, increased defense spending even at the cost of cutting domestic programs, and support of the Equal Rights Amendment. The aggregate differences between southern and nonsouthern Fundamentalists are almost as large on questions relating to developing nuclear power more rapidly, taking stronger action to reduce inflation even if it increases unemployment, cutting nondefense spending to balance the budget, and instituting a government-sponsored national health insurance program. These variations are not surprising because they are generally consistent with the bulk

TABLE 5.4

Political Philosophy of State Party Activists, Controlling for Region and Fundamentalism
(in percent)

Political Philosophy	Southern		Nonsouthern	
	Fundamentalist	Non-Fundamentalist	Fundamentalist	Non-Fundamentalist
Very liberal	2	8	5	15
Somewhat liberal	8	20	20	31
Middle-of-the-road	13	17	18	18
Somewhat conservative	33	36	34	26
Very conservative	44	20	24	10
Total	100	101	101	100
(N)	(1,145)	(2,480)	(1,270)	(5,005)

Source: Compiled by the authors from state party convention delegate data.

TABLE 5.5

Issue Positions of White State Party Activists by Fundamentalism/Non-Fundamentalism, Controlling for Region (in percent)

Issue and Position*	Southern		Nonsouthern	
	Fundamentalist	Non-Fundamentalist	Fundamentalist	Non-Fundamentalist
"New politics" or social issues				
Equal Rights Amendment				
Favor	19	44	40	64
Undecided	8	8	10	9
Oppose	73	48	50	27
Total	100	100	100	100
(N)	(1,152)	(2,514)	(1,282)	(5,133)
Constitutional amendment to prohibit abortions except when the mother's life is in danger				
Favor	60	21	54	26
Undecided	11	11	11	9
Oppose	29	68	35	66
Total	100	100	100	101
(N)	(1,150)	(2,497)	(1,278)	(5,127)
Affirmative action programs in jobs and in higher education				
Favor	24	36	32	44
Undecided	19	16	25	22
Oppose	57	48	43	34
Total	100	100	100	100
(N)	(1,130)	(2,483)	(1,253)	(5,073)
More rapid development of nuclear power				
Favor	72	58	53	41
Undecided	16	18	21	18
Oppose	12	24	26	40
Total	100	100	100	99
(N)	(1,129)	(2,478)	(1,278)	(5,139)

(continued)

TABLE 5.5 (continued)

Issue and Position*	Southern		Nonsouthern	
	Fundamentalist	Non-Fundamentalist	Fundamentalist	Non-Fundamentalist
Economic issues				
Government-sponsored national health insurance program				
Favor	16	26	29	39
Undecided	12	15	12	14
Oppose	72	59	60	47
Total	100	100	101	100
(N)	(1,133)	(2,498)	(1,053)	(4,179)
Deregulation of oil and gas prices				
Favor	55	58	51	45
Undecided	21	20	22	23
Oppose	24	22	27	32
Total	100	100	100	100
(N)	(1,102)	(2,461)	(1,263)	(5,057)
Stronger action to reduce inflation even if it increases unemployment substantially				
Favor	60	56	45	42
Undecided	20	19	22	21
Oppose	20	25	33	37
Total	100	100	100	100
(N)	(1,102)	(2,432)	(1,249)	(5,037)
Across-the-board cuts in nondefense spending to balance the budget				
Favor	73	59	57	44
Undecided	9	12	13	15
Oppose	18	29	30	41
Total	100	100	100	100
(N)	(1,136)	(2,486)	(1,262)	(5,097)
Mandatory wage and price controls to deal with inflation				
Favor	29	27	30	34
Undecided	15	15	18	19

Oppose	56	58	52	47
Total	100	100	100	100
(N)	(1,112)	(2,441)	(1,274)	(5,087)

Foreign policy and defense issues

An increase in defense spending even if it means cutting domestic programs

Favor	87	70	66	48
Undecided	6	10	13	13
Oppose	7	19	21	40
Total	100	99	100	101
(N)	(1,151)	(2,501)	(1,276)	(5,126)

Ratification of SALT II

Favor	15	29	27	44
Undecided	16	18	20	21
Oppose	68	53	53	35
Total	99	100	100	100
(N)	(1,089)	(2,417)	(1,242)	(5,052)

Reinstituting draft registration

Favor	80	73	69	55
Undecided	8	9	11	11
Oppose	12	18	19	34
Total	100	100	99	100
(N)	(1,121)	(2,448)	(1,276)	(5,121)

Increasing U.S. military presence in the Middle East

Favor	76	62	54	41
Undecided	16	21	26	24
Oppose	8	17	20	35
Total	100	100	100	100
(N)	(1,115)	(2,461)	(1,253)	(5,079)

*The "strongly favor" and "mildly favor" responses checked by respondents on these questionnaire items have been combined to yield the "favor" percentages in this table; similarly, the "strongly oppose" and "mildly oppose" responses have been combined to yield the "oppose" percentages. Percentages do not always total 100 because of rounding.

Source: Compiled by authors from state party convention delegate data.

TABLE 5.6

Issue Positions of White Southern and Nonsouthern State Party
Activists Correlated with Fundamentalism

	Southern	Nonsouthern
"New politics" or social issues		
Equal Rights Amendment	-.20	-.20
Antiabortion amendment	.30	.25
Affirmative action	-.06	-.09
Nuclear power development	.10	.12
Economic issues		
National health insurance	-.09	-.06
Deregulation of oil and gas	-.02	.05
Reduce inflation	.02	.03
Balance budget	.09	.08
Wage and price controls	.01	-.02
Foreign policy/defense issues		
Increase in defense spending	.14	.15
Ratification of SALT II	-.12	-.14
Draft registration	.08	.10
Military in Middle East	.12	.10

Source: Compiled by the authors from state party convention
data.

of earlier research. However, in order to understand better the Fundamentalist impact on southern politics, it is also important to compare patterns of Fundamentalist/non-Fundamentalist issue positions within each of the two regional categories.

To some degree, the initial observation of interregional differences is modified by two other observations that put the patterns of responses in Table 5.5 into clearer perspective. First, within each region the Fundamentalist delegates are consistently more conservative—although in some cases only slightly so—than the non-Fundamentalist delegates, and in virtually every case the within-region intergroup differences are almost identical. Within the context of the politics of the respective regions, then, Fundamentalistm apparently has a roughly similar influence: it tends to make the delegates more conservative. The correlation coefficients reported in Table 5.6 give general support to this point in demonstrating almost no regional variations in the relationship between Fundamentalism and delegates' issue positions. Moreover, in each region this relationship is strongest on essentially the same social and foreign policy issues and weakest on the same economic issues.

The second moderating observation is that on nine of the thirteen issues southern non-Fundamentalists are slightly more conservative than nonsouthern Fundamentalists. Although these differences are generally quite small, they indicate nevertheless that the issue positions examined here are related at least to some degree to regional factors independent of religious Fundamentalism. Further confirmation is presented in Table 5.7, which reports correlation coefficients for the relationship between issue positions and region along with first-order partial correlations for the relationship controlling for Fundamentalism. On 12 of the 13 issues the relationship between delegates' issue positions and region is stronger than the rela-

TABLE 5.7

Issue Positions of White Southern and Nonsouthern State Party Activists Correlated with Region: Zero-Order and First-Order Partial Correlations Controlling for Fundamentalism

	Zero-Order Correlations	First-Order Partials
"New politics" or social issues		
Equal Rights Amendment	-.25	-.23
Antiabortion amendment	.03	.00
Affirmative action	-.14	-.13
Nuclear power development	.21	.20
Economic issues		
National health insurance	-.15	-.14
Deregulation of oil and gas	.12	.12
Reduce inflation	.16	.16
Balance budget	.17	.16
Wage and price controls	-.08	-.08
Foreign policy/defense issues		
Increase defense spending	.27	.26
Ratification of SALT II	-.19	-.18
Draft registration	.19	.18
Military in Middle East	.25	.24

Source: Compiled by the authors from state party convention data.

tionship between these issue positions and Fundamentalism (compare with Table 5.6). The only exception concerns the antiabortion amendment, where Fundamentalism exhibits a stronger relationship than region (.03 for region compared with .27 for Fundamentalism without the regional controls included in Table 5.6). In addition, the introduction of Fundamentalism as a control for the relationship between region and these issue positions has almost no effect in reducing the magnitude of the zero-order correlations (see Table 5.7).[20]

In brief, southern white Fundamentalists are more consistently conservative both in general political philosophy and in specific policy orientations than nonsouthern white Fundamentalists. At the same time, however, southern Fundamentalists do not differ substantially from nonsouthern Fundamentalists in their qualitative impact on the regional political systems in which they are active. In both the southern and nonsouthern states included in this study, white Fundamentalist activists are about equal to the political Right of non-Fundamentalist delegates and therefore they occupy a comparable position within their respective systems. Although we can identify some interregional differences between the two groups of Fundamentalist activists, we are quickly forced to modify the conclusion by observing that within an intraregional context they differ very little from each other in the aggregate. Furthermore, other regional factors (whose identification lies beyond the scope of this chapter) emerge ultimately as being more closely related than Fundamentalist religion to these delegates' policy preferences.

CANDIDATE PREFERENCES OF ACTIVISTS

Delegates' feelings toward the six leading presidential contenders at the time of the 1980 state conventions conform to the same basic pattern as that described in the previous section. Of the six contenders, Kennedy, Brown, Reagan, and Anderson projected fairly clear ideological images. In each of these four instances two points stand out clearly. First, southern Fundamentalists are more favorable to the most conservative candidate (Reagan) and less favorable to the more liberal candidates (Kennedy, Brown, and Anderson) than nonsouthern Fundamentalists (see Table 5.8). This is, of course, consistent with the greater policy conservatism of southern Fundamentalist party leaders demonstrated earlier in this chapter. Second, again in conformity with the distribution of opinions on ideology and issues, Fundamentalists in each broadly defined region are more favorable to Reagan and less favorable to Kennedy, Brown, and Anderson than non-Fundamentalists. These intraregional differences show marked similarity in magnitude, a point further confirmed by the cor-

TABLE 5.8

Candidate Orientations of White State Party Activists by
Fundamentalism/Non-Fundamentalism, Controlling for Region
(in percent)

Candidate Orientation	Southern		Nonsouthern	
	Funda-mentalist	Non-Funda-mentalist	Funda-mentalist	Non-Funda-mentalist
Jimmy Carter				
Favorable	29	36	35	35
Neutral	3	3	4	4
Unfavorable	68	61	60	61
Total	100	100	99	100
(N)	(1,158)	(2,495)	(1,276)	(5,082)
Edward Kennedy				
Favorable	6	16	19	31
Neutral	3	4	4	6
Unfavorable	91	80	77	62
Total	100	100	100	99
(N)	(1,101)	(2,453)	(1,265)	(5,045)
Jerry Brown				
Favorable	3	7	9	17
Neutral	7	11	11	15
Unfavorable	90	83	80	68
Total	100	101	100	100
(N)	(1,082)	(2,429)	(1,230)	(4,948)
Ronald Reagan				
Favorable	75	54	53	34
Neutral	4	4	5	5
Unfavorable	21	42	41	62
Total	100	100	99	101
(N)	(1,099)	(2,446)	(1,253)	(4,990)
George Bush				
Favorable	41	49	44	40
Neutral	16	17	16	17
Unfavorable	43	34	40	43
Total	100	100	100	100
(N)	(1,057)	(2,403)	(1,210)	(4,902)
John Anderson				
Favorable	11	26	25	41
Neutral	16	19	20	19
Unfavorable	73	55	55	40
Total	100	100	100	100
(N)	(1,044)	(2,398)	(1,205)	(4,884)

Note: Percentages do not always total 100 because of rounding.

Source: Compiled by the authors from state party convention delegate
data.

TABLE 5.9

Candidate Orientations of White Southern and Nonsouthern State
Party Activists Correlated with Fundamentalism

Candidate	Southern	Nonsouthern
Jimmy Carter	-.01	.02
Edward Kennedy	-.12	-.10
Jerry Brown	-.10	-.11
Ronald Reagan	.16	.15
George Bush	-.10	-.01
John Anderson	-.14	-.15

Source: Compiled by the authors from state party convention
data.

relation coefficients listed in Table 5.9. This leads to two observations:

1. Within the context of regional politics Fundamentalism has an essentially similar effect in qualitative terms as it has within the context of specific issues: it tends to make delegates more conservative.

TABLE 5.10

Candidate Orientations of White Southern and Nonsouthern State
Party Activists Correlated with Region: Zero-Order and First-
Order Partial Correlations Controlling for Fundamentalism

Candidate	Zero-Order Correlations	First-Order Partials
Jimmy Carter	-.03	-.03
Edward Kennedy	-.22	-.21
Jerry Brown	-.20	-.19
Ronald Reagan	.22	.21
George Bush	.05	.06
John Anderson	-.20	-.18

Source: Compiled by the authors from state party convention
data.

2. Apparently, some regional factors independent of Fundamentalism help to account for the differences between southern and nonsouthern delegates reported in Table 5.8.

Both points receive support from the data in Table 5.10 illustrating that region correlates more strongly with candidate orientations (at least for the four more clearly classified contenders) than Fundamentalism does and that the introduction of Fundamentalism as a control variable has only a negligible effect on the zero-order correlations.

In a sense, the data on attitudes toward Carter and Bush fall outside this pattern. Analysis of these orientations is more difficult partly because both candidates were hard to categorize ideologically and partly because feelings toward Carter involve various other considerations (for example, his southern background, his publicly professed religious Fundamentalism, and his incumbency). Under these circumstances, it is hardly surprising that no clear connections between Fundamentalism and orientations toward Carter and Bush emerge.

For the data that can be analyzed, the same conclusions apply as for ideology and issues. That is, while southern Fundamentalists are more conservative in their candidate preferences than nonsouthern Fundamentalists, they differ very little within an intraregional context, and evidently other regional factors are more strongly related than Fundamentalist religion to activists' feelings toward candidates.

CONCLUSION

In some ways, the data presented in this chapter serve to reduce the mystique of southern religion and its connection to regional politics. At least as far as party activists are concerned, southern and nonsouthern Fundamentalists generally resemble each other in aggregate personal and political background characteristics. Although they differ somewhat in educational background, income levels, and denominational affiliations, and a bit more sharply in party-identification patterns and levels of political campaign activity, they are essentially similar on other background points. While southern Fundamentalists tend to be more Republican and more intensely active than nonsouthern Fundamentalists, both tend to be primarily middle-aged, somewhat disproportionately more representative of males than females, mainly from small-town and rural areas, and fairly stable residentially. Moreover, both groups have been involved in party work for remarkably similar periods and, as revealed by their patterns of motivations for party work, for very similar reasons. Also, on most

of the background variables examined, southern and nonsouthern
Fundamentalists differ from non-Fundamentalists in their respective
regions in the same general ways. On balance, then, there is relatively little in their backgrounds to differentiate Fundamentalist activists by region.

At first glance, their respective positions on ideological and issue questions and their candidate preferences appear to change this
picture considerably, as southern Fundamentalists consistently take
more conservative positions and more strongly favor conservative
candidates and oppose liberal candidates than nonsouthern Fundamentalists. This may be a reflection of their different patterns of denominational and partisan affiliations. However, more detailed considerations advance the analysis one step further and suggest that, with the
exception of the abortion issue, these Fundamentalist activists are
again quite similar in relative position within their political systems
(as shown by comparisons with non-Fundamentalist activists) and
that the initial policy and candidate differences they display are related to regional factors other than those specifically connected with
religion. In both the southern and nonsouthern states in our study,
the Fundamentalist delegates give the political system a more conservative cast, but in the South the white party elites simply have a
more conservative center of gravity to begin with.

These findings do not negate the importance of religion generally or Fundamentalism specifically in the study of southern politics.
They do suggest that the impact of Fundamentalism on southern politics differs from its impact on nonsouthern politics more because of
quantitative differences than because of qualitative differences. In
other words, the combination of greater numbers of Fundamentalists
in the South and their higher levels of political activity there seems
to do more than any inherent doctrinal differences to account for the
differential influence on regional politics found in other studies. In
these terms our data underscore the continuing importance of Fundamentalism (and religion in general) in the study of southern politics.
Certainly the topic is worthy of further research, which could include other states, other organizational levels of party activists, and
other political elites.

NOTES

1. Here Fundamentalism is defined in terms summarized by
Thomas R. Ford as follows: "The core of fundamentalism is Bibli-
cism, or belief in the inerrancy of the literally interpreted Scriptures.
Built around this core are various creedal tenets: the Virgin Birth,
Christ's miracles, physical resurrection, and others. There is also

an ethical aspect of fundamentalism that is popularly referred to as 'Puritan morality.'" See Thomas R. Ford, "Status, Residence, and Fundamentalist Religious Beliefs in the Southern Appalachians," Social Forces 39 (October 1960): 41. See also the definitional discussions of Fundamentalism in Gordon F. DeJong and Thomas R. Ford, "Religious Fundamentalism and Denominational Preference in the Southern Appalachian Region," Journal for the Scientific Study of Religion 5 (October 1965): 24-43; and David C. Moberg, The Church as Social Institution: The Sociology of American Religion (Englewood Cliffs, N.J.: Prentice-Hall, 1962), pp. 282-83.

2. See, for example, the election report in Congressional Quarterly Almanac, vol. 36 (Washington, D.C.: Congressional Quarterly, 1980). For a more general treatment, see Gerald Pomper, ed., The Election of 1980: Reports and Interpretations (Chatham, N.J.: Chatham House, 1981), especially p. 51.

3. For example, Jerry Falwell, leader of the Moral Majority, has claimed success in defeating various targeted candidates. See Congressional Quarterly Almanac, vol. 36 (Washington, D.C.: Congressional Quarterly, 1980), p. 8B.

4. In addition to earlier chapters in this book addressing the question rather directly, see the general discussion of the 1980 elections in Paul R. Abramson, John H. Aldrich, and David W. Rohde, Change and Continuity in the 1980 Elections (Washington, D.C.: Congressional Quarterly, 1982). The entire book provides an excellent background for consideration of specific questions concerning the election.

5. Michael Parenti, "Political Values and Religious Cultures: Jews, Catholics, and Protestants," Journal for the Scientific Study of Religion 6 (Fall 1967): 266-67; Charles Y. Glock and Robert Wuthnow, "Departures from Conventional Religion: The Nominally Religious, the Nonreligious, and the Alternatively Religious," in The Religious Dimension: New Directions in Quantitative Research, ed. Robert Wuthnow (New York: Academic Press, 1979), pp. 64-67; William A. McIntosh, Letitia T. Alston, and Jon P. Alston, "The Differential Impact of Religious Preference and Church Attendance on Attitudes toward Abortion," Review of Religious Research 20 (Spring 1979): 195-213; and Rodney Stark and Charles Y. Glock, American Piety: The Nature of Religious Commitment (Berkeley and Los Angeles: University of California Press, 1968).

6. David R. Morgan and Kenneth J. Meier, "Politics and Morality: The Effect of Religion on Referenda Voting," Social Science Quarterly 61 (June 1980): 144-48; and David Fairbanks, "Religious Forces and 'Morality' Politics in the American States," Western Political Quarterly 30 (September 1977): 411-17.

7. Theodore C. Wagenaar and Patricia E. Bartos, "Orthodoxy and Attitudes of Clergymen toward Homosexuality and Abortion," Review of Religious Research 18 (Winter 1977): 114-25; Larry R. Peterson and Armand L. Mauss, "Religion and the 'Right to Life': Correlates of Opposition to Abortion," Sociological Analysis 37 (Fall 1976): 243-54; James T. Richardson and Sandie Wightman, "Religious Affiliation as a Predictor of Voting Behavior in Abortion Reform Legislation," Journal for the Scientific Study of Religion 11 (December 1972): 347-59; James T. Richardson and Sandie Wightman Fox, "Religion and Voting on Abortion Reform: A Follow-up Study," Journal for the Scientific Study of Religion 14 (June 1975): 159-64; Bradley Hertel, Gerry E. Hendershot, and James W. Grimm, "Religion and Attitudes toward Abortion: A Study of Nurses and Social Workers," Journal for the Scientific Study of Religion 13 (March 1974): 23-34; Ted Jelen, "Sources of Political Intolerance: The Case of the American South," in Contemporary Southern Political Attitudes and Behavior, ed. Laurence W. Moreland, Tod A. Baker, and Robert P. Steed (New York: Praeger, 1982), pp. 73-91; and McIntosh, Alston, and Alston, "Attitudes toward Abortion," pp. 195-213.

8. Charles H. Anderson, White Protestant Americans: From National Origins to Religious Group (Englewood Cliffs, N.J.: Prentice-Hall, 1970), chap. 12; John J. Hutcheson, Jr., and George Taylor, "Religious Variables, Political System Characteristics, and Policy Outputs in the American States," American Journal of Political Science 17 (May 1973): 414-21; Joe R. Feagin, "Prejudice and Religious Types: A Focused Study of Southern Fundamentalists," Journal for the Scientific Study of Religion 4 (October 1964): 3-13; Fred W. Grupp, Jr., and William M. Newman, "Political Ideology and Religious Preference: The John Birch Society and Americans for Democratic Action," Journal for the Scientific Study of Religion 12 (December 1973): 401-12; T. C. Keedy, "Anomie and Religious Orthodoxy," Sociology and Social Research 43 (September-October 1958): 34-37; W. Seward Salisbury, "Religiosity, Regional Sub-Culture, and Social Behavior," Journal for the Scientific Study of Religion 2 (October 1962): 94-101; Roland Robertson, The Sociological Interpretation of Religion (New York: Schocken Books, 1970), chap. 6, especially p. 184; and Murray S. Stedman, Jr., Religion and Politics in America (New York: Harcourt, Brace & World, 1964), p. 13.

For material suggesting that the link between Fundamentalism and prejudice, anti-Semitism, and so forth is not so clear, see among others, Roy Lotz, "Another Look at the Orthodoxy—Anti-Semitism Nexus," Review of Religious Research 18 (Winter 1977): 126-33; Ronnie R. Strickland and Sallie Cone Waddell, "Religious Orientation, Racial Prejudice, and Dogmatism: A Study of Baptists and Unitarians," Journal for the Scientific Study of Religion 11 (December 1972): 395-99;

and C. Daniel Batson, Stephen J. Naifeh, and Suzanne Pate, "Social Desirability, Religious Orientation, and Racial Prejudice," Journal for the Scientific Study of Religion 17 (March 1978): 31–41.

9. Robertson, The Sociological Interpretation of Religion, p. 184; and Stedman, Religion and Politics in America, chap. 6.

10. Harold E. Quinley, "The Dilemma of an Activist Church: Protestant Religion in the Sixties and Seventies," Journal for the Scientific Study of Religion 13 (March 1974): 1–21; Ernest Q. Campbell and Thomas F. Pettigrew, "Racial and Moral Crisis: The Role of the Little Rock Ministers," American Journal of Sociology 64 (March 1959): 509–16; and Samuel S. Hill, Jr., Southern Churches in Crisis (New York: Holt, Rinehart & Winston, 1966), chaps. 5 and 7.

11. Hill, Southern Churches in Crisis, chap. 2.

12. John Shelton Reed, The Enduring South: Subcultural Persistence in a Mass Society (Lexington, Mass.: D. C. Heath, Lexington Books, 1971); James R. Shortridge, "A New Regionalization of American Religion," Journal for the Scientific Study of Religion 16 (June 1977): 143–53; and Wilbur Zelinsky, "An Approach to the Religious Geography of the United States: Patterns of Church Membership in 1952," Annals of the Association of American Geographers 51 (1961): 139–93. See also David E. Sopher, Geography of Religions (Englewood Cliffs, N.J.: Prentice-Hall, 1967); and Edwin S. Gaustad, "Religious Demography of the South," in Religion and the Solid South, ed. Samuel S. Hill, Jr. (Nashville, Tenn.: Abingdon Press, 1972), pp. 143–78.

13. Shortridge, "A New Regionalization," p. 151.

14. Jelen, "Sources of Political Intolerance," pp. 73–91.

15. Salisbury, "Religiosity," pp. 94–101.

16. Ibid., especially p. 97.

17. See, for example, Robertson, The Sociological Interpretation of Religion, especially p. 184; Campbell and Pettigrew, "Racial and Moral Crisis," pp. 509–16; Stedman, Religion and Politics in America, chap. 6; Franklin H. Littell, From State Church to Pluralism: A Protestant Interpretation of Religion in American History (Garden City, N.Y.: Doubleday, 1962), pp. 147–56; William B. Hesseltine, The South in American History (Englewood Cliffs, N.J.: Prentice-Hall, 1936), pp. 624–28; and Samuel S. Hill, Jr., "The South's Two Cultures," in Religion and the Solid South, ed. Samuel S. Hill, Jr. (Nashville, Tenn.: Abingdon Press, 1972), pp. 24–56.

18. Activists, for example, tend to be more tolerant, more supportive of civil liberties, and so forth than the mass public. For a summary of studies in this vein, see Lester W. Milbrath and M. L. Goel, Political Participation: How and Why Do People Get Involved in Politics? 2d ed. (Chicago: Rand McNally, 1977), pp. 144–48.

19. See, among others, Joseph R. Washington, Jr., Black Religion: The Negro and Christianity in the United States (Boston: Beacon

Press, 1964); Liston Pope, "The Negro and Religion in America," Review of Religious Research 5 (Spring 1963): 142-52; Hart M. Nelsen and Anne Kusener Nelsen, Black Church in the Sixties (Lexington: University of Kentucky Press, 1975); Benjamin E. Mays and Joseph W. Nicolson, The Negro's Church (New York: Institute of Social and Religious Research, 1933); and Hart M. Nelsen, Raytha L. Yokley, and Thomas W. Madron, "Ministerial Roles and Social Actionist Stance: Protestant Clergy and Protest in the Sixties," American Sociological Review 38 (June 1973): 384.

20. Controlling for political party and religion (Fundamentalism) at the same time reduces the strength of the relationship between delegates' issue positions and region, but even this does not eliminate the regional effect altogether. Second-order partials not reported here show this to be especially true for certain issues such as support for the Equal Rights Amendment, increased defense spending, more rapid development of nuclear power, draft registration, and increased U.S. military presence in the Middle East.

6

FUNDAMENTALIST BELIEFS AND SOUTHERN DISTINCTIVENESS: A STUDY OF THE POLITICAL ATTITUDES OF STATE PARTY ACTIVISTS

Tod A. Baker
Robert P. Steed
Laurence W. Moreland

INTRODUCTION

Southern distinctiveness or southernness is a topic that has long preoccupied a number of scholars. One school of thought, illustrated by the work of Numan Bartley and John Shelton Reed, develops its theory of southernness on the concept of the sectional mind—a set of attitudes and values that tend to distinguish Southerners from non-Southerners. [1] Since this viewpoint asserts that Southerners can be considered an ethnic or ethnocultural group, with values and beliefs transmitted on an intergenerational basis, the South as a distinctive region will endure even though it has been profoundly transformed by urbanization, industrialization, the emergence of party competition, and the civil rights movement.

The second school of thought, well represented by V. O. Key, Jr., and I. A. Newby, has built its theory of southern distinctiveness on foundations provided by the South's distinctive institutions—white supremacy, the one-party system, poverty, illiteracy, and small-town, rural society. [2] As stated by Newby:

> It has been argued implicitly throughout this study that southernness was an ideology extruded by a distinctive way of life which grew in turn from a specific set of circumstances. If that argument is valid, southernness and thus the South, cannot long survive the destruction of the way of life . . . that expressed it and the set of circumstances that produced it. . . . [W]riters who speak hopefully of an enduring South are basing their hope not on fundamental features but on vestigial remains. [3]

Although southern religious beliefs and practices, including Fundamentalism, should certainly be included in any catalog of southern subcultural traits—see the previous chapter, for example[4]—several observers have asserted that in the South religious institutions, practices, and beliefs have tended to support and maintain what has been referred to as the traditional southern way of life. Newby, for example, has noted that religious beliefs in the South have tended to reflect secular values rather than mold them;[5] Joseph Fichter and George Maddox have pointed out that "it may be said without disrespect that the churches seem to employ God to maintain and retain the Old South";[6] and Reed has stated that "it appears that most Southern churches are . . . so much a part of the community as to be indistinguishable from it."[7] Samuel Hill has developed this notion more fully.

> Tersely stated, religion is dominantly a conservative or reinforcing agent for the traditional values held by white southern society. Pattern-maintenance has been the primary result, if not the declared intention. Granted, some prophetic activity has taken place. Nevertheless the overall impact of the church leadership has been priestly in that secular traditions and values have been "baptised" and accorded legitimacy. [8]

Therefore, an important function of religion has been to maintain orthodox southern values and beliefs, that is, southern distinctiveness.

DATA AND METHODOLOGY

This chapter seeks to measure the degree to which the religious beliefs of party activists in South Carolina and Virginia tend to support distinctively southern political attitudes. On the assumption that Fundamentalist beliefs tap the southernness dimension, respondents are classified in terms of a Fundamentalist/non-Fundamentalist dichotomy. The dependent variables are seven issues that can be considered as distinctively southern.

In addition to the religious distinction, party activists are also classified according to partisan identification and race. In terms of party identification, it seems plausible to assume that the growth in the appeal of Republicanism to Southerners should be of some significance in sorting people out along liberal or conservative lines. Therefore, if for this set of party activists partisan ideology is indeed the principal line of cleavage on the seven issues, it will indicate that southern politics is in the process of becoming nationalized; that is, the pattern of two-party competition characteristic of the national level and found in many states has begun to penetrate the South. [9] Religious beliefs, therefore, should have reduced significance in maintaining orthodox southern values.

It also seems plausible to assume that the emergence of blacks as politically relevant actors could affect the relationship between religious beliefs and southernness. Whereas the white church in the South has tended to reflect dominant viewpoints and hence has taken a conservative position, the black church, which has also been characterized by Fundamentalist beliefs, has tended to strike a much more progressive note, beginning long before the civil rights movement of the post-World War II period. [10] Thus the black church has a long history of commitment to change. Given this background, black Fundamentalists should take a nonsouthern position on the seven issues, indicating that the movement of blacks into the Democratic party elite is, at least, moderating the relationship between Fundamentalism and southernness.

Issues

The seven issues studied here include four about military affairs and three about minority rights. [11]

The military affairs issue area encompasses a proposal to increase defense spending even if it means cutting domestic programs, ratification of the SALT II treaty, reinstitution of draft registration, and increased U.S. military presence in the Middle East. A relatively large body of literature indicates that Southerners tend to take a generally favorable attitude toward the military. John Hope Franklin, for example, described the evolution of the military tradition in the South from 1800 to 1861, [12] and Alfred O. Hero continued the analysis into the post-World War II period. [13] Other observers also have developed this viewpoint. William C. Havard has asserted that Southerners tend to be characterized by a "military-patriotic" outlook, [14] and Newby has noted that Southerners tend to be more in favor of a strong U.S. position in world affairs than non-Southerners. [15] Charles P. Roland, writing about the Vietnam War, stated that "southerners and their political leaders remained into the 1970s perhaps the most dedicated of all American advocates of the unilateral employment of arms, keeping alive a vestigial spirit of 'going it alone' to police the world."[16]

The minority rights issue area encompasses the Equal Rights Amendment (ERA), a proposal calling for a constitutional amendment to prohibit abortions except when the mother's life is threatened, and affirmative action programs in jobs and higher education. Because all three issues apply to women—the third is also applicable to blacks—they can be classified within the frame of reference of traditional southern attitudes toward women. Although the traditional image of the southern lady as submissive, intuitive, nonlogical, tactful, sympathetic, and innocent was probably never completely accurate, it has nevertheless continued to shape perceptions of southern womanhood. [17] Thus, as Fowlkes, Perkins, and Rinehart pointed out, "When the southern lady did emerge in politics—as she did in the latter part of the nineteenth century . . . —she did so with a style and flair as consistent with the myth as possible." [18] And Roland noted that "southern women in the 1960s and 1970s harkened to the practical aspects of the Women's Liberation Movement. . . . But they did not renounce either their femininity or their southernness. They retained enough of what William Alexander Percy once called a 'morning-glory air' to make a southern Bella Abzug impossible to imagine." [19]

Hence the southern position is defined as one opposed to the ERA, in favor of the constitutional amendment to prohibit abortions, and opposed to affirmative action. In addition, since traditional southern politics could be described as the politics of color, opposition to affirmative action is also consistent with traditional attitudes toward race relations.

Methodology

Our study examines the positions of six groups—white Fundamentalist Democrats, white non-Fundamentalist Democrats, black Fundamentalist Democrats, black non-Fundamentalist Democrats, white Fundamentalist Republicans, and white non-Fundamentalist Republicans—on the seven issues discussed in the previous section. [20] Discriminant analysis is employed. This technique allows simultaneous analysis of the differences between two or more groups with respect to two of more variables. [21] Our procedure is to examine the discriminant functions and the classification matrix to determine the variables that are dominant on each function, and to analyze the group means on each function.

A discriminant function is evaluated in terms of its capacity to distinguish between groups. [22] Two statistics, the relative percentage and the canonical correlation, are utilized to ascertain a function's substantive significance. The relative percentage is based on the eigenvalue and measures the discriminating power of a function relative to other functions. [23] The canonical correlation, on the other hand, is a test of the strength of the relationship between a given function and the groups. Thus it provides information that the relative percentage cannot give. [24]

The capacity to predict group memberships correctly is an additional method for testing for the degree of group separation. As such it is a measure of the discriminating power in the variables.[25]

In addition, the variables that are dominant on a given function determine the information that the function carries, that is, they can be used to name it. This can be accomplished through the use of standardized discriminant-function coefficients or through the use of zero-order correlations between the individual variables and the function. The latter method is employed here.[26]

Finally, the group means indicate the position of each group on a given function. These means are expressed in standard-deviation units from the grand mean.[27] Since the variables in this study were coded from nonsouthern or liberal to southern or conservative, a negative score indicates a nonsouthern position and a positive score indicates a southern one.

DISCUSSION

The eigenvalues, relative percentages, and canonical correlations for the five functions are depicted in Table 6.1. This table reveals that only the first two functions possessed a relatively substantial amount of discriminating power, with the first function accounting for 79.17 percent of the variance and the second for 17.17 percent. The canonical correlations on the first two functions indicate that a moderate-to-strong relationship exists between the function and the groups.

TABLE 6.1

Discriminating Power of the Discriminant Functions

Function	Eigenvalue	Relative Percent of Variance	Canonical Correlation
1	1.26758	79.17	.7476639
2	0.27491	17.17	.4643617
3	0.04234	02.64	.2015405
4	0.01383	00.86	.1167971
5	0.00249	00.16	.0498303

Source: Compiled by the authors.

TABLE 6.2

Pooled Within-Groups Correlations between the Canonical
Discriminant Functions and the Discriminating Variables

Discriminating Variable	Function 1	Function 2
Equal Rights Amendment	.69949	.14340
SALT II	.66938	.16140
Affirmative action	.66494	-.44630
Increased defense spending	.65522	-.03937
Reinstituting draft registration	.24662	.00689
Increasing U.S. military presence in Middle East	.23493	.14947
Constitutional amendment to abolish abortion	.26886	.81543

Source: Compiled by the authors.

With regard to the capacity to predict group memberships correctly, the classification matrix indicates that the groups are well
separated. Overall, 52.79 percent of the grouped cases were classified correctly, with the percentage classified correctly for each group
as follows: white Fundamentalist Democrats, 37.0 percent; white
non-Fundamentalist Democrats, 49.5 percent; black Fundamentalist
Democrats, 48.7 percent; black non-Fundamentalist Democrats, 52.2
percent; white Fundamentalist Republicans, 62.7 percent; and white
non-Fundamentalist Republicans, 54.3 percent. This is a considerable improvement over the 16.67 percent probability of group assign-
ment on a random basis.

In terms of the information carried by each function, four issues
are dominant on the first function and one on the second (see Table
6.2). The four dominant issues on the first function are drawn from
both issue areas and include the Equal Rights Amendment, ratification
of the SALT II treaty, the affirmative action proposal, and the proposal
calling for an increase in defense spending. The abortion issue is
dominant on the second function. Whereas the first function could be
thought of as tapping a generalized southernness dimension inasmuch
as issues from both issue areas are dominant, the second seems to
tap that facet of southern distinctiveness that could be thought of as
constituting a moral dimension.

In terms of the group means, on the first function party ideology is the basic cleavage between delegates, with Democrats taking the nonsouthern position and Republicans the southern one (see Table 6.3). Race is also important inasmuch as blacks, both Fundamentalist and non-Fundamentalist, took the most extreme nonsouthern positions. Whereas religious beliefs were of some importance in separating the groups (for each of the three pairs of delegates Fundamentalists were more southern than non-Fundamentalists), the major thrust tends to support the Key-Newby viewpoint on southern distinctiveness; changes in distinctively southern institutions—that is, the emergence of blacks as politically relevant actors and the transformation of the one-party system—have affected the relationship between religious beliefs and distinctively southern political attitudes.

On the other hand, the group means on the second function suggest that, for moral issues, the emergence of party competition and the movement of blacks into the political elite may not have affected the relationship between religious beliefs and southernness. On the abortion function white Fundamentalist Democrats, white Fundamentalist Republicans, and blacks took the southern position; white non-Fundamentalist Democrats and white non-Fundamentalist Republicans took the nonsouthern one. Indeed, blacks who were the most nonsouthern on the first function were the most southern on the abortion function.

The significance of these results depends, of course, on the relationship of the abortion issue to other moral issues. If abortion is unrelated to other moral issues, it can simply be handled on an ad hoc basis as an issue that simply refuses to fall into the pattern. However, if the abortion issue does lie on the same dimension as other moral issues (such as school prayer, gay rights, and legalization of

TABLE 6.3

Canonical Discriminant Functions Evaluated at Group Means

Group	Function 1	Function 2
White Fundamentalist Democrats	−0.43746	0.19109
White non-Fundamentalist Democrats	−1.25550	−0.37401
Black Fundamentalist Democrats	−1.62649	1.33541
Black non-Fundamentalist Democrats	−1.76819	0.94175
White Fundamentalist Republicans	1.21394	0.58407
White non-Fundamentalist Republicans	0.87383	0.35208

Source: Compiled by the authors.

liquor, pornography, and gambling), then it may well be that for issues of this type increasing party competition will not result in the replacement of religious beliefs with partisan identification as the basis for decision. Also, within the Democratic party the movement of blacks into the political elite could shift the party in a more conservative or southern orientation.

CONCLUSION

Obviously, the development of party competition and the emergence of blacks as politically relevant actors have affected the relationship between Fundamentalist beliefs and distinctively southern political attitudes, at least within the ranks of party activists. The Key-Newby position appears correct inasmuch as the dissolution of two traditional southern institutions, the one-party system and racial segregation, has resulted in the emergence of partisan ideology and race as basic lines of cleavage among members of the political elite. Yet, the group means on the second (the abortion) function suggest that whereas Fundamentalism tends not to undergird southern distinctiveness in general, it may be quite salient for issues dealing with moral questions.[28] A point of possible significance is that blacks, who in line with the literature on the progressive nature of the black church took the most nonsouthern position on the first function, took the most southern position on the second function. Recently, Merle Black and John Shelton Reed have presented evidence rather strongly suggesting that southern blacks have begun to think of themselves as Southerners.[29] In terms of their position on the abortion issue, blacks may be the most southern group of all.

Whereas at least at the present it appears unlikely that on the national level moral issues will supplant economic, military, or foreign policy issues as topics of dominant concern, it may well be that in southern states and communities issues such as abortion, pornography, school prayer, gambling, and legalization of liquor might occupy the center ring of political discourse.[30] If this does occur, then for at least one set of issues the relationship between religious beliefs and political attitudes will be relatively unaffected by the development of party competition. Assuming that both parties continue to recruit white non-Fundamentalists, it appears unlikly that either party will be able to take a position on moral issues. Furthermore, the movement of blacks into the Democratic elite could result in the creation of a black wing that is strongly conservative or southern on moral issues. This too could tend to immobilize the Democratic party.

NOTES

1. Numan V. Bartley, "The South and Sectionalism in Southern Politics," Journal of Politics 38 (August 1976): 257; John Shelton Reed, The Enduring South: Subcultural Persistence in a Mass Society (Lexington, Mass.: D. C. Heath, Lexington Books, 1972); and John Shelton Reed, One South: An Ethnic Approach to Regional Culture (Baton Rouge: Louisiana State University Press, 1982).

2. V. O. Key, Jr., Southern Politics in State and Nation (New York: Alfred A. Knopf, 1949); and I. A. Newby, The South: A History (New York: Holt, Rinehart & Winston, 1978).

3. Newby, The South: A History, p. 507.

4. See also Reed, The Enduring South, chap. 6.

5. Newby, The South: A History, p. 410.

6. Joseph Fichter and George Maddox, "Religion in the South, Old and New," in The South in Continuity and Change, ed. John C. McKinney and Edgar T. Thompson (Durham, N.C.: Duke University Press, 1965), p. 383.

7. Reed, The Enduring South, p. 72.

8. Samuel S. Hill, Jr., "The South's Two Cultures," in Religion and the Solid South, ed. Samuel S. Hill, Jr. (Nashville, Tenn.: Abingdon Press, 1972), p. 36. See also Reed, The Enduring South, pp. 69-72.

9. For a discussion of the nationalization of the party system in Virginia, see Alan I. Abramowitz, John McGlennon, and Ronald Rapoport, "Presidential Activists and the Nationalization of Politics in Virginia," in Contemporary Southern Political Attitudes and Behavior, ed. Laurence W. Moreland, Tod A. Baker, and Robert P. Steed (New York: Praeger, 1982), pp. 183-96.

10. See Joseph R. Washington, Jr., Black Religion: The Negro and Christianity in the United States (Boston: Beacon Press, 1964), especially chaps. 2-3; Liston Pope, "The Negro and Religion in America," Review of Religious Research 5 (Spring 1963): 142-52; and Hart M. Nelson and Anne Kusener Nelson, Black Church in the Sixties (Lexington: University of Kentucky Press, 1975).

11. The five economic issues and one nuclear power issue discussed in the previous chapter were not covered here because they do not fall within the meaning of southern distinctiveness. With regard to the economic issues, Key found in his 1961 study that the attitudes of Southerners tended not to differ from those of non-Southerners. See V. O. Key, Jr., Public Opinion and American Democracy (New York: Alfred A. Knopf, 1961), pp. 103-4. The nuclear power issue is simply too recent an issue to be fitted within the frame of reference of southern distinctiveness.

12. John Hope Franklin, The Militant South: 1800-1861 (Cambridge, Mass.: Belknap Press, 1956).

13. Alfred O. Hero, The Southerner and World Affairs (Baton Rouge: Louisiana State University Press, 1965), chap. 3.

14. William C. Havard, ed., The Changing Politics of the South (Baton Rouge: Louisiana State University Press, 1972), p. 6.

15. Newby, The South: A History, p. 468.

16. Charles P. Roland, The Improbable Era: The South since World War II (Lexington: University Press of Kentucky, 1975), p. 90.

17. See Anne Firor Scott, The Southern Lady from Pedestal to Politics: 1830-1930 (Chicago: University of Chicago Press, 1970), chap. 1.

18. Diane L. Fowlkes, Jerry Perkins, and Sue Tolleson Rinehart, "Women in Southern Party Politics: Roles, Activities, and Futures," in Party Politics in the South, ed. Robert P. Steed, Laurence W. Moreland, and Tod A. Baker (New York: Praeger, 1980), pp. 214-32.

19. Roland, The Improbable Era, p. 179.

20. The number of respondents for each group are as follows: white Fundamentalist Democrats, 268; white non-Fundamentalist Democrats, 999; black Fundamentalist Democrats, 160; black non-Fundamentalist Democrats, 100; white Fundamentalist Republicans, 667; white non-Fundamentalist Republicans, 1,189. Since there were only 30 black Republicans, these activists were excluded from the analysis.

21. William R. Klecka, Discriminant Analysis (Beverly Hills: Sage, 1980), p. 7.

22. A discriminant function is a linear combination of discriminating variables that maximizes the difference between group means. Once the first function has been derived, additional ones are derived subject to the constraint that the values on each given function are uncorrelated with the values on the others. The maximum number of functions that can be derived is equal to the number of groups minus one, or in the event that there are fewer variables than groups, the number of variables. See ibid., pp. 16-18.

23. The sum of the eigenvalues is a measure of the total variance in the discriminating variables. Thus a single eigenvalue, expressed as a percentage of the total sum of eignevalues, is a measure of that eigenvalue's relative importance. See Klecka, Discriminant Analysis, pp. 35-36.

24. Ibid., pp. 36-38.

25. Ibid., pp. 49-51.

26. For a discussion of the advantages of the structure matrix over the matrix of discriminant function coefficients, see ibid., pp. 29-34.

27. Ibid., pp. 22-23.

28. On this point see Chapter 4 of this book.

29. Merle Black and John Shelton Reed, "Blacks and Southerners: A Research Note," Journal of Politics 44 (February 1982): 165-71.

30. See Paul R. Abramson, John H. Aldrich, and David W. Rhode, Change and Continuity in the 1980 Elections (Washington, D.C.: Congressional Quarterly Press, 1982), pp. 121-22.

7

VIRGINIA: A CASE STUDY OF FUNDAMENTALISM IN STATE PARTY POLITICS

Alan Abramowitz
John McGlennon
Ronald Rapoport

INTRODUCTION

The impact of religious belief on politics has been a subject of considerable interest to political observers in recent years. A resurgence of Evangelical Christianity and the organization of Fundamentalist Christians to accomplish political goals has raised a series of questions regarding the impact and consequences of religious involvement in politics.

While this religious reawakening has been a nationwide phenomenon, the South has seemed to be especially receptive to it. Religious Fundamentalism is more widespread in the largely Protestant South.[1] John Shelton Reed has provided compelling evidence that religion is more central to the lives of Southerners than other Americans.[2]

In addition, much of the movement to encourage political involvement by Fundamentalist and Evangelical Christians originated with southern churches and ministers such as Jerry Falwell of Lynchburg, Virginia, James Robison of Fort Worth, Texas, and Jim Bakker of Charlotte, North Carolina.

Religion has played a significant role in elections throughout U.S. history, of course. Religiously inspired abolitionists were among the supporters of the Republican party's first successful presidential candidate, Abraham Lincoln.[3] Intolerance toward Catholicism became an issue in several nineteenth-century campaigns for president and other offices. In the South the presidential candidacies of Catholics Al Smith in 1928 and, to a lesser extent, John Kennedy in 1960 caused cracks in the "solid" Democratic vote. In both cases, however, the candidates were also the beneficiaries of strong support from their coreligionists.[4]

In 1976 the question of religious tolerance was reversed for many traditional Democratic voters. Not only did their party nominate a Deep South candidate for president, but it nominated a candidate who had openly discussed his rebirth and his strong religious beliefs. Jimmy Carter was a former lay Baptist missionary; his religious roots probably won him support among rural Protestant voters even in northern states such as Ohio, Pennsylvania, and Iowa, but it also made traditional Catholic and Jewish urban Democrats uneasy.[5] Carter went to great lengths in his postnomination campaign and during his administration to assure voters that his religion was a personal matter that would not determine his policy choices.

The 1980 election found religion once again moving to the forefront of the presidential campaign. The two major party nominees and the most popular Independent candidate declared themselves to be born again. Although the candidates again insisted their religious beliefs would not determine their policy initiatives as president, Fundamentalist ministers began to organize Christians as a coherent political force to influence the outcome of the elections for president, Congress, and other offices.

Jerry Falwell took the lead in developing an organization dedicated to instilling Fundamentalist values (as he saw them) in the political system.[6] This organization, known as the Moral Majority, became a rallying point for conservative Fundamentalists, a symbol of reaction to political liberals and the theological mainstream, and in many places, a cause for concern by longtime political party leaders fearful of a party takeover by an organized, intensely committed band of religious zealots.[7]

RELIGIOUS INVOLVEMENT IN POLITICAL PARTIES

If religion has always played an important part in this nation's electoral politics, why did the involvement of Fundamentalist Christians in 1980 seem to arouse so much interest? Two factors can best explain this concern: the prior lack of political interest among this group and the nature of the political processes they were involving themselves in.

The social characteristics of Fundamentalists, who are disproportionately rural, less educated, less affluent, and more southern than non-Fundamentalists, are generally associated with lack of political involvement and interest.[8] Mobilization of this group to attain political goals would be a remarkable accomplishment and would provide the potential for a significant impact on some elections. The first major tests of Fundamentalist influence would be in circumstances likely to exaggerate the effect of their political organization.

The nominating processes by which the two major political parties select their presidential candidates have undergone major changes in response to complaints of unresponsiveness in the 1968 selection. Particularly as a result of criticism by opponents of the Vietnam War who claimed their influence in the Democratic party's selection process was restrained by nominating rules, the Democrats approved major reforms in time for the 1972 nominations.[9] The most significant impacts of these reforms have been to permit participation in the nominating process by anyone willing to claim membership in the party regardless of past participation in or support for the party, and to require proportional representation in the selection of delegates to local, state, and national conventions. In effect, the winner-take-all system was discouraged or even prohibited, especially in states using mass meetings or caucuses to select delegates.

The effects of these changes were seen almost immediately, as George McGovern was able to take a well-organized constituency, the antiwar movement, and pack mass meetings across the country with supporters of his candidacy. McGovern's ability to mobilize this group was matched by his inability to broaden his support in the electorate at large, and he suffered one of the worst electoral defeats in U.S. presidential history. Still, his campaign showed the distortion made possible by the new rules, which were generally adopted by both parties.[10]

In fact, though, even under the old rules states using the caucus-convention method of selection for national convention delegates had always been vulnerable to well-organized minority groups. The nomination of Barry Goldwater by the Republican party in 1964 was aided substantially by the disproportionate success of Goldwater supporters in these states, which typically had a much smaller rate of participation than states holding primaries. If Fundamentalist Christians were going to have an impact on the selection of 1980 presidential candidates, their chances were much greater in the caucus-convention states.

This chapter examines two cases in which Fundamentalist Christians sought to influence the outcome of nomination contests. In the first case, although they were ultimately unsuccessful, Fundamentalists had a distorting impact on the 1978 nomination and election contests for the U.S. Senate in Virginia. In the second case, the impact of Fundamentalist delegates in Virginia's 1980 Republican state convention is examined to determine whether the call of several influential television ministers for greater involvement in the nominating process by their followers significantly affected the outcome of the conventions.

Virginia has the distinction of being the one state in the nation to move away from the primary as the preferred method of nomination for statewide offices in recent years. Since 1978 Virginia Democrats have nominated by convention two U.S. Senate candidates and candi-

dates for governor, lieutenant governor, and attorney general, the
only statewide offices elected in Virginia. Republicans have used
the direct primary only once in this century to nominate a statewide
candidate. Abandonment of the direct primary by Virginia Democrats
stemmed directly from the party's failure to win any election for
governor or U.S. Senate from 1969 to 1977. The Democrats' failure
was attributed largely to the division created within the party by bitter
primary contests between liberal and conservative candidates. These
contests not only alienated significant portions of the party's traditional
supporters, but also consumed large amounts of monetary and organizational resources. For example, in 1969 liberal Democrats helped
elect Virginia's first Republican governor in nearly a century as an
expression of dissatisfaction with the outcome of the Democratic primary. In 1977 the success of the liberal candidate drove tens of
thousands of conservative Democrats to support the Republican nominee. One panel survey of voters in the 1977 primary found that 90
percent of the loser's supporters voted for the Republican candidate
in the general election. [11]

Since adopting the convention method, the Democrats have lost
two U.S. Senate races (in 1978 and 1982), but by very narrow mar-
gins. In 1981 they swept the three state offices, the first time either
party has done so since 1965.

DATA

The data used in this study are drawn from surveys conducted
at both the Democratic and Republican state conventions in Virginia
in 1978 and 1980. In 1978 a sample of delegates to each state convention was asked to complete a six-page, self-administered questionnaire. Approximately one-third of the sample did so, yielding 422
Democratic responses and 421 Republican responses. In 1980 all
delegates were asked to complete a similar questionnaire. Some
1,716 Republicans and 1,669 Democrats did so, resulting in responses
from slightly more than half of the delegates at each convention. In
the case of the 1978 delegates, a follow-up survey was mailed to all
respondents after the November election. Approximately 75 percent
of the delegates responded to this second survey. No follow-up was
conducted among the 1980 delegates.

The 1980 survey was part of a larger, 11-state comparative
study of political party activists coordinated by the authors of this
chapter. Comparisons of Virginia delegates with nonsouthern
delegates are based on the survey results in Arizona, Colorado, Iowa,
Maine, and North Dakota.

Fundamentalist Involvement in the 1978
U.S. Senate Race

In 1978 eight Democrats sought their party's nomination for a
U.S. Senate seat, which was to become vacant due to retirement.[12]
Delegates were selected in mass meetings across the state, with
proportional representation for any candidate attaining the support
of 15 percent of a locality's caucus attendance. Four Republicans
pursued their party's nomination, but for them there was no require-
ment of proportionality. Unit-rule and plurality winner-take-all systems were permitted. The differences in the methods used by Democrats and Republicans probably accounted for some of the impact
of Fundamentalist Christians in the Democratic nominating contest.

One Democratic candidate, a Norfolk city councilman who had
previously been uninvolved in Democratic politics at either the city
or state level, announced eight weeks before the mass meetings that
he had been "told by God" to run for the Senate as a Democrat. This
was apparently something of a surprise even to the candidate, who
admitted he had always thought of himself as more of a Republican.
Still, with only two months to organize a statewide campaign, candidate Conoly Phillips and his campaign manager, Virginia Beach television evangelist Pat Robertson ("The 700 Club"), worked through
ministers and churches in several parts of the state to turn out large
groups of supporters on the day of the mass meetings. As a result
of their efforts, Phillips won the third largest set of delegates to the
convention—about 16 percent—and actually dominated the selection
process in several cities and counties in the state's tidewater region.

Even Democratic activists who had seen the full impact of the
McGovern movement in Virginia were unprepared for the invasion
of the Phillips supporters. In some localities the party's mass meetings were turned into virtual revival meetings, with prayer sessions
and rhythmic clapping and chanting. Church buses carried literally
hundreds of Fundamentalists, many of whom had never been registered to vote before, to participate in their first political meeting.
Phillips himself acknowledged the unusual character of his campaign
in a tape recording sent to all convention delegates in which he frankly
stated that "most Democrats had already committed themselves to
other candidates. So we had to turn to Christians for support." Not
all the delegates appreciated the assumption of mutual exclusivity
between Christianity and the Democratic party.

The mass meeting itself had alienated a good number of Democratic activists, who either found themselves in delegations dominated by political novices with no obvious ties to the party or were
actually denied a place at the convention by the novices' success. In
some sense this was no different than what confronted long-time

Democrats of the Byrd machine in 1972, when party leaders like former Governor Mills Godwin were denied seats at the state convention by local mass meetings packed by supporters of George Mcgovern's presidential campaign. Still, the 1972 insurgents had been fairly politically involved prior to their success. They included liberals, members of organized labor, minority voters, and antiwar activists who had been involved in political matters for some time, even if not always successfully. This could not be said of the Fundamentalists in 1978.

Like their candidate, few of the Phillips delegates had any previous involvement in Democratic party politics. In fact, many had never been involved in politics before, and a majority considered themselves to be either Independents or Republicans. They were chosen as delegates because of their leadership positions in their churches. They were far more conservative, less educated, and more likely to have migrated to Virginia than other Democratic delegates.

There were also sharp differences in the motivations of the Phillips and other Democratic delegates. Two of every five Phillips delegates cited religious or moral convictions as their reason for becoming convention delegates, while only one other Democratic delegate sought election for the same reason. And these delegates attended the convention because of Conoly Phillips's candidacy. While 34 percent of the other delegates sought election because of their support for a particular candidate, 43 percent of the Phillips candidates were there primarily to nominate Phillips.

Within the Virginia Democratic party, already plagued with internal division and antagonisms, the Phillips delegates were not entirely comfortable. A plurality of the Phillips delegation actually had voted for Republican candidates in the preceding two statewide elections. Many had not even voted. In both 1976 and 1978 Phillips delegates had an abstention rate four times higher than the nonvoting rates of other delegates.

More than anything else, the moral attitudes of the Phillips delegates, rooted in the Fundamentalist, rigidly conservative preaching of their churches, identified them politically. They were monolithically opposed to the Equal Rights Amendment (90 percent), legalization of marijuana (87 percent), and federal funding of abortions (93 percent). However, this overwhelming conservatism did not always carry over into their attitudes toward economic and social issues. On questions such as wage-price controls, defense spending, tax reform, and deregulation of natural gas, the Phillips delegates generally fell between the Democratic convention delegates and the Republicans.

The success of the Phillips candidacy was limited, of course. A veteran Democrat, who had narrowly lost the 1977 gubernatorial

primary and had twice before won statewide elections, was nominated
on the third ballot. But the impact of the Phillips delegates on the
Democrats in 1978 was powerful. Although they had taken one-sixth
of the seats at the state Democratic convention, these Fundamentalists
showed little interest in the party's needs. Some party leaders talked
bravely of drawing this new and potentially important group of supporters to the Democrats, but the Phillips supporters had come to
the convention fully expecting him to be nominated despite his obvious
lack of support among the overwhelming majority of delegates. Few
were prepared for the defeat, which was obvious on the first ballot
and final after the third. They left the convention in disbelief, unwilling to commit themselves to future party involvement.

The lack of commitment to the Democratic party among the
Phillips supporters was not surprising, given their dislike of most
of the party's state and national leaders. While 98 percent of the
Conoly Phillips delegates felt "very favorable" toward him, a majority
of them gave favorable ratings only to then-President Jimmy Carter
from among numerous Democratic officeholders and candidates. The
president's strong Southern Baptist religious background undoubtedly
helped his standing in this group, which also rated Republican Ronald
Reagan more favorably than either then Lieutenant Governor Charles
Robb, Senator Edward Kennedy, former Lieutenant Governor Henry
Howell, or any of the other Senate candidates. Many Phillips delegates, in some cases a plurality, were unable to express any opinion
about political leaders.

The single-minded approach of the Phillips delegates was also
evident in their unwillingness to consider other contenders. Nearly
three out of every five Phillips supporters indicated they could not
support at least one of the other candidates, and most of them named
the eventual nominee, a moderate who had done nothing in particular
to alienate them other than to win more delegates than their favorite.
The other delegates returned the compliment: of the 55 percent who
indicated they could not support some other candidate for the party
nomination, two-thirds singled out Conoly Phillips.

Attitudes like these effectively ended the possibility that involvement in a common political experience might encourage further attempts by the Phillips delegates to participate in Democratic party
politics. As the postelection survey demonstrated, their involvement
in the general election campaign in support of the eventual nominee
was minimal. While 75 percent of the Phillips delegates indicated
they planned to remain active in the party when surveyed at the convention (but before the nominations), only 35 percent said they would
remain when resurveyed after the election.

Still, the 1978 study made it clear that conditions for ongoing
involvement by religiously motivated delegates might be found under

another set of circumstances. The Phillips delegates were isolated in the Virginia Democratic party, and their candidate was unsuccessful.

This contest presented the parties with a cause for concern over the capricious involvement of a special-interest group in party activities. At the same time, it may have presented a worst-case scenario. It involved a late-starting, inexperienced candidate and supporters who joined a party in which they did not belong and in which opposition to their attitudes existed on a number of important political issues. Their involvement in 1980 might present an entirely different effect.

Fundamentalist Participation in the 1980
Presidential Nominations in Virginia

Concern over Fundamentalist involvement in the nominating process generally stems from fear that a highly organized group, representing only a small portion of the electorate, will seize a party nomination from a more representative nominee, thereby weakening the party both organizationally and electorally. [13] Nominations for public office are frequently decided by small fractions of the total potential electorate. An organized minority can exert disproportionate influence over such a selection when mobilized behind a particular candidate. When that minority is distinctly different in its orientation from other participants in the nominating process, tension and disruption of the party are likely to occur. Such a situation developed in the Virginia Senate nomination.

In contrast to the 1978 phenomenon, involvement of Fundamentalists in the presidential nominating conventions of 1980 was generally seen as part of a wider movement in the Republican party nationally toward a more conservative posture and presidential candidate. While Conoly Phillips's Democratic delegates found few natural allies in the Senate convention, such a group was more likely to feel at home in a Republican party that had moved to the right after the 1976 elections. Still, the participation of Fundamentalists both individually and as part of a nationally organized movement raised questions of their effects on the political process in general and on political party activists in particular.

The presence of substantial numbers of Fundamentalist Christian delegates in the nominating process of the two major political parties in Virginia should not be surprising, given the concentration of the more Fundamentalist and Evangelical religious sects in the South. Still, given the lower socioeconomic levels and political interest of Fundamentalist Christians, it would not be surprising to find this group underrepresented among political activists.

TABLE 7.1

Selected Social Characteristics of Virginia
Republican Delegates
(in percent)

Characteristics	Fundamentalist	Non-Fundamentalist
Age		
18–30	15	15
30–45	36	32
45–60	32	36
60 or older	17	18
Total	100	101
(N)	(490)	(1,060)
Education		
None to some high school	5	1
High school graduate	14	7
Some college	33	29
College graduate	20	28
Post-graduate	28	35
Total	100	100
(N)	(495)	(1,073)
Income		
$0-$15,000	14	7
$15,000-$25,000	24	17
$25,000-$45,000	41	45
$45,000 or more	22	31
Total	101	100
(N)	(457)	(1,005)

Note: Percentages do not always total 100 because of rounding.
Source: Compiled by the authors from Virginia convention data.

If born-again or Fundamentalist Christians wanted to affect
presidential nominating politics as a group in 1980, they should have
been united in their point of view (being relatively new to politics),
and they should have organized within one party in support of one
candidate. Fundamentalist political organizers made it clear early

in the campaign that they intended to participate within the Republican party for the purpose of nominating a socially conservative candidate for president.

In 1980 the measure used in our survey was a simple self-description by the delegates of whether they were Fundamentalist or born-again Christians. As expected, Fundamentalists were much more likely to be found in Virginia than in nonsouthern state conventions. Among Democrats, 38 percent of the Virginians were Fundamentalists whereas only 12 percent of non-Southerners were Fundamentalists. Of course a substantial number of these Democratic Fundamentalists were blacks. More than two-thirds of black Virginia Democrats described themselves as Fundamentalists, but only 28 percent of white Virginia Democrats did so.

Among Republicans, regional differences were not as great but did exist. In any case, Republican conventions had a somewhat higher rate of Fundamentalist involvement than did Democratic conventions, and the South had higher levels of such participation than did non-southern states. Of those born again, 42 percent were southern Republicans and 26 percent were nonsouthern Republicans. In Virginia, 32 percent called themselves Fundamentalist.

The presence of substantial numbers of Fundamentalist delegates in the Republican conventions in the South, particularly, created the potential for the kind of problems the Democrats had faced in Virginia in 1978. In fact, a far larger portion of the seats were occupied by Fundamentalists in the 1980 Virginia Republican conventions than had been held by Conoly Phillips delegates in 1978. But the character of these delegates was markedly different from the unique experience of the Virginia Democrats. As in 1978, the Republican Fundamentalists in 1980 tended to be younger, were less educated, and had lower incomes than non-Fundamentalist delegates (see Table 7.1).

These delegates were also welcomed much more readily in the Virginia Republican party. On the morning the convention was to select Virginia's national convention delegates, early arrivals were greeted by an official entertainment program featuring the "Sounds of Liberty," a patriotic singing group from Jerry Falwell's Liberty Baptist College.

A major cause of concern to party leaders over the involvement of Fundamentalist Christians in the nominating process was that these delegates would be politically inexperienced and uninvolved and would be replacing loyal, active party workers. That had been the case in the 1978 Democratic convention. However, these delegates provided a substantially different picture. Fundamentalist Republicans of the 1980 convention had been involved in the political process. Virginia's Fundamentalist Republicans were only slightly less likely than their non-Fundamentalist brethren to have been delegates to previous con-

TABLE 7.2

Party Activity of Virginia Republican Delegates
(in percent)

Activity	Fundamentalist	Non-Fundamentalist
Member, local party committee	48	56
(N)	(496)	(1,074)
Delegate to previous convention	56	65
(N)	(494)	(1,071)
Active in all or most recent campaigns	60	67
(N)	(489)	(1,070)

Source: Compiled by the authors from Virginia convention data.

TABLE 7.3

Pragmatism of Virginia Republican Delegates
(in percent)

	Fundamentalist	Non-Fundamentalist
Strongly agree that parties should be primarily concerned with promoting issues rather than winning elections	54	33
(N)	(474)	(1,030)
Strongly agree that it is better for party to lose than to compromise its principles	63	45
(N)	(469)	(1,034)
Strongly disagree that a party should seek broad appeal among voters rather than ideological purity	51	36
(N)	(464)	(1,021)

Source: Compiled by the authors from Virginia convention data.

ventions, to have served on local party committees, or to have been active in political campaigns. Fundamentalists of the 1980 Republican convention were not likely to have the same impact on party organization as the Conoly Phillips delegates had. First-time Fundamentalist delegates could find congenial fellow delegates who might encourage them to maintain their activity in future elections (see Table 7.2).

Although Fundamentalist delegates had been involved in politics before, they still might have an orientation toward politics that could set them apart from their more secular counterparts. Fundamentalists might be expected to prefer parties to maintain a consistent ideology than to develop broad electoral appeal. Dogmatism in matters of faith might be expected to transfer to matters of politics as well. In fact, Fundamentalist Republican delegates were somewhat less pragmatic than other Republicans (see Table 7.3).

Opinion surveys of Fundamentalist Christians have generally found this group to be somewhat more conservative than others. The differences are not extreme, however. The same can be said of delegates to the 1980 Republican conventions on economic and national security issues (see Table 7.4). Overall, Fundamentalist delegates were more conservative than non-Fundamentalists, but only slightly so. Fundamentalists did vary significantly on issues closely associated with morality and religious tenets, the Equal Rights Amendment, and abortion. But in general, as other analyses have shown, far greater differences occurred across party lines and within parties across regions.[14] Nonsouthern delegates, whether born again or not, tended to be more liberal than Virginia Republicans, whether Fundamentalist or not.

The presence of significant numbers of Fundamentalist delegates at the 1980 southern Republican convention does not seem to have significantly affected the party's operation. These Fundamentalist activists had been involved in their party in the past and could be expected to continue their activity in the future. In contrast to the Fundamentalist invasion of the Virginia Democratic convention in 1978, these delegates felt ideologically comfortable in their parties. Still, there was one area in which a large number of Fundamentalist delegates, united in purpose and acting as a bloc, might have a disproportionate influence on their party: in the selection of the nominee for president.

Fundamentalist political action groups concentrated their attention on the Republican party in 1980, and as evidenced by their numbers in state conventions, they met with some success. More important, these Fundamentalist delegates seemed remarkably united in their candidate preference. Of course Ronald Reagan was the overwhelming favorite of all Republican convention delegates. In the state conventions surveyed nationally he held a 78-to-13-percent ad-

156 / RELIGION AND POLITICS IN THE SOUTH

TABLE 7.4

Issue Differences among Fundamentalist and Non-Fundamentalist
Republican Delegates in Virginia
(in percent)

Issue	Fundamentalist	Non-Fundamentalist
Equal Rights Amendment		
Oppose	85	71
(N)	(486)	(1,063)
Antiabortion amendment		
Favor	67	28
(N)	(487)	(1,062)
Increase defense spending		
Favor	92	93
(N)	(488)	(1,062)
Domestic spending cuts		
Favor	74	75
(N)	(479)	(1,056)
Affirmative action		
Oppose	65	70
(N)	(480)	(1,057)
More nuclear power		
Favor	75	76
(N)	(474)	(1,054)

Source: Compiled by the authors from Virginia convention data.

vantage among Fundamentalists over his closest competitor, George
Bush, compared with a 60-to-26-percent lead among other Republicans.

In Virginia Reagan was extremely popular, especially among
Fundamentalists. He won the support of 87 percent of them, while
only 69 percent of non-Fundamentalists named him as their preference.
To a large degree the born-again effect in the Republican nominating
contest appears to be a function of both region and religion. The
South was particularly hospitable to Reagan's appeal, and the predominant religions of the South contain fairly high concentrations of
Fundamentalists. However, even controlling for religion, a Fundamentalist effect remains: Fundamentalist delegates were more supportive of Reagan than were their coreligionists in the major church
groupings (see Table 7.5).

TABLE 7.5

Candidate Preferences of Virginian Republican Delegates
(in percent)

Candidate	Baptist		Methodist		Catholic		Other Christian	
	Fun-damen-talist	Non-Fun-damen-talist	Fun-damen-talist	Non-Fun-damen-talist	Fun-damen-talist	Non-Fun-damen-talist	Fun-damen-talist	Non-Fun-damen-talist
Reagan	86	76	91	61	96	76	82	65
Bush	4	11	8	28	0	14	10	20
Other	10	13	1	11	4	10	8	15
Total	100	100	100	100	100	100	100	100
(N)	(221)	(75)	(64)	(188)	(27)	(174)	(164)	(576)

Source: Compiled by the authors from Virginia convention data.

Fundamentalist Christians did seem to play a significant role in the Republican nominating process. In Virginia, where they comprised 42 percent of the delegates, Fundamentalists were especially important. Their impact on the nominating process, however, is somewhat more problematic. As conservatives they were at home in the Republican party, especially in Virginia. As supporters of Ronald Reagan they were in tune with the overwhelming preference of their nonsouthern and non-Fundamentalist fellow delegates. Their impact at the Virginia state convention did not change the outcome but only made it more emphatic.

CONCLUSION

The 1978 Virginia Democratic convention and the involvement of Fundamentalist Christians in it demonstrated the potential for mischief in religiously inspired political party involvement. Similar situations and other well-publicized attempts to use religious belief and organizations in partisan politics had created a sense of concern as the 1980 election began. The outcome of the 1980 Virginia Republican convention reflected such involvement.

If Fundamentalist political groups had a distorting effect on the 1980 presidential nominating contest, that effect is not evident in the data presented here. Although Fundamentalist Christians (especially southern Republicans) participated in both parties' conventions, it would be hard to argue that they were overrepresented. Nor does it appear that these Fundamentalists were invading the political process in a kind of holy crusade. Most were experienced political activists who were continuing their involvement in their preferred party.

Still, Fundamentalists did differ in some ways from other members of their own party, even if some differences were largely owing to regional variations in the party. The born-again Republican delegates of 1980 were satisfied with the nomination of their preferred candidate for president. As a result, they could be expected to play an active role in the fall campaign. Had they failed, the consequences for the Republican party could have been severe. Given the relative lack of pragmatism among Fundamentalist delegates and their strong moral stance on issues such as abortion, the nomination of a more moderate candidate might have led to a significant degree of disaffection among Republican delegates. That these delegates had been among the party's recent activists might in fact have exacerbated the problem for the Republicans. Whether or not continued involvement in party activity can indeed moderate the dogmatism of Fundamentalist Christian delegates is a question worth pursuing.

NOTES

1. See, for instance, Monroe Lee Billington, The Political South in the Twentieth Century (New York: Charles Scribner's Sons, 1975), pp. 44-55; and Murray S. Stedman, Jr., Religion and Politics in America (New York: Harcourt, Brace & World, 1964). For recent survey data on religious affiliation and Fundamentalism in the South, see the Gallup Organization, Religion in America, 1981 (Princeton, N.J.: Gallup Opinion Index, 1981), p. 61.

2. John Shelton Reed, The Enduring South: Subcultural Persistence in a Mass Society (Lexington, Mass.: D.C. Heath, Lexington Books, 1972).

3. Cushing Strout, The New Heavens and New Earth: Political Religion in America (New York: Harper & Row, 1974), pp. 140-43; and James L. Sundquist, Dynamics of the Party System (Washington, D.C.: Brookings Institution, 1973), pp. 40-43.

4. Sundquist, Dynamics of the Party System, pp. 176-82.

5. Gerald Pomper, ed., The Election of 1976: Reports and Interpretations (New York: David McKay, 1977), p. 63; and Albert J. Menendez, Religion at the Polls (Philadelphia: Westminster Press, 1977), pp. 102-3.

6. For a valuable discussion of this movement, see Michael Lienesch, "Right-Wing Religion: Christian Conservatism as a Political Movement," Political Science Quarterly 97 (Fall 1982): 403-25.

7. See, for example, "A Tide of Born-Again Politics," Newsweek, September 15, 1980, pp. 28-36; and George J. Church, "Politics from the Pulpit," Time, October 13, 1980, pp. 28-35.

8. Philip E. Converse, "On the Possibility of Major Party Realignment in the South," in Elections and the Political Order, ed. Angus Campbell, Philip E. Converse, Warren E. Miller, and Donald E. Stokes (New York: John Wiley & Sons, 1966), pp. 223-24.

9. For a fuller discussion of these reforms and their effects, see James I. Lengle, Representation and Presidential Primaries (Westport, Conn.: Greenwood Press, 1981); Thomas R. Marshall, Presidential Nominations in a Reform Age (New York: Praeger, 1981); Terry Sanford, A Danger of Democracy (Boulder, Colo.: Westview Press, 1981); and Steven E. Schier, The Rules and the Game (Washington, D.C.: University Press of America, 1980).

10. Marshall, Presidential Nominations, p. 177.

11. Alan Abramowitz, John McGlennon, and Ronald Rapoport, "Voting in the Democratic Primary: The 1977 Virginia Gubernatorial Race," in Party Politics in the South, ed. Robert Steed, Tod Baker, and Laurence Moreland (New York: Praeger, 1980), pp. 91-94.

12. For a fuller discussion of Virginia's 1978 senatorial election, see Alan Abramowitz, John McGlennon, and Ronald Rapoport,

Party Activists in Virginia: The 1978 Senatorial Nominating Conventions (Charlottesville, Va.: Institute of Government, 1981).

13. Austin Ranney, "The Political Parties: Reform and Decline," in The New American Political System, ed. Anthony King (Washington, D.C.: American Enterprise Institute, 1979), p. 240.

14. For a discussion of the interparty differences among Fundamentalist and non-Fundamentalist delegates, see Robert P. Steed, Laurence W. Moreland, and Tod A. Baker, "Religion and Politics: Fundamentalism among State Party Activists" (Paper presented at the Conference on State Party Elites, College of William and Mary, Williamsburg, Va., October 1-3, 1981). Data on regional differences within parties are presented in Alan Abramowitz, John McGlennon, and Ronald Rapoport, "Fundamentalism and Southern Party Elites: Born Again Christians in the 1980 Presidential Nominating Process" (Paper presented at the Third Citadel Symposium on Southern Politics, The Citadel, Charleston, South Carolina, March 25-27, 1982), table 3.

8

PREACHERS AND POLITICS:
VARIETIES OF ACTIVISM
AMONG SOUTHERN
BAPTIST MINISTERS

James L. Guth

Within the past five years a widening split has appeared within the nation's largest Protestant denomination, the Southern Baptist Convention. Religious and political conservatives identified with the so-called New Christian Right have lobbied to put the Southern Baptist Convention (SBC) on record against theological liberalism and in favor of Christian Right political positions. These activities have elicited counterorganization by moderates and liberals. And although the battle has continued since at least 1978, neither side has established clear dominance. Little is known about the distribution of opinion on major issues, the identity of the warring parties, or prospects for Christian Right politics in the Southern Baptist Convention. [1]

In an effort to answer some of these questions, a nine-page, 110-item questionnaire was sent to a random sample of Southern Baptist ministers drawn from approximately 40,000 pastors listed in the "SCB 1980 Convention Annual." Questions sought to elicit the ministers' opinions on political issues of special concern to the Christian Right; on their social, educational, and political histories; on their feelings about political activism by ministers; on their own political involvement; and on their relationships with their congregations, other ministers, and the SBC itself. Because of the unexpected timing of the study, the necessity of quick completion, and the desire for comparability with other studies of laymen and ministers, many questions were drawn from earlier work by Jeffrey Hadden, Harold Quinley, and national polling organizations. [2]

Questionnaires were mailed on November 14, 1980. After one follow-up letter and two additional mailings, the survey finally elicited 460 usable responses. Returns indicated that at least 16 members of the original sample had died or left the ministry. Thus the response rate for the reduced sample of 740 was 62.2 percent, comparable to or better than many similar studies of ministers.[3] Evidence from the survey itself and from postal returns indicates that Southern Baptist ministers are very mobile and that many of them probably never received the survey instrument. Still, comparison of respondents with Southern Baptist ministers as a whole (by means of information gleaned from various issues of the SBC Quarterly Review) indicates that those who returned the questionnaire are quite representative, with the possible exception of being slightly better educated. Thus there is no reason to suspect that response bias is an insuperable problem for interpretation and analysis.

The ministers in this survey are essentially southern ministers, even though the Southern Baptist Convention includes congregations outside the South. Of the ministers in the sample over 85 percent are currently stationed in the South (inclusive of border states), and almost all of these were born in the South. Of the sample about 95 percent were either born in the South or are stationed in the South.

Southern Baptist ministers are deeply divided in their reactions to the Christian Right. Only a handful were actually members of organizations such as Moral Majority (3 percent, N = 14), but another 43 percent (N = 197) had "heard about and generally approved" of Moral Majority. Yet another 47 percent (N = 216) had "heard about and generally disapproved" of the organization, while 7 percent (N = 33) had not heard about it or could not or would not evaluate it. An earlier article reported that members and sympathizers were drawn disproportionately from certain sectors of the Southern Baptist clergy. By theological identity, Fundamentalists (25 percent of the total) favored Moral Majority by a 2-to-1 margin, conservatives (59 percent of the total) were evenly divided, moderates (15 percent of the total) voted 4-to-1 against the organization, and liberals (less than 1 percent of the sample) were uniformly opposed. Comparable splits appeared between political conservatives (72 percent of the sample) and moderates (26 percent of the sample). Republicans (27 percent of the total) approved of Moral Majority by a wide margin (56 percent approving and 34 percent disapproving), while Independents (27 percent of the total) were closely divided and Democrats (45 percent of the total) firmly rejected the organization (39 percent approving and 54 percent disapproving). Moral Majority supporters were drawn from the ranks of blue-collar and farm-reared ministers, from those with modest or intermediate levels of education (usually from conservative seminaries), and from pastors disenchanted with the organizational life of the Southern Baptist Convention.[4]

A second article focused on political activism. Given the slight numerical advantage of the Moral Majority's foes, why does the Christian Right faction appear to dominate Southern Baptist clerical involvement in political life? The answer proved to be quite complex but can be summarized as follows: Christian Rightists among Southern Baptist ministers have extremely positive attitudes toward involvement in politics, actually participate at a much higher level and in more visible acts, and generally serve congregations that are more supportive—or at least more tolerant—of ministerial political activism. [5]

In this chapter the focus shifts to the distribution of Southern Baptist ministerial opinion on various political issues. Unfortunately, not all the questions a political scientist might like to ask could be incorporated in an already lengthy survey instrument. However, an effort was made to include queries representative of Christian Right concerns on government and the economy, on the nature of political ideology and Christian belief, on defense and foreign policy, and on various social issues. We were especially interested in the overall distribution of ministerial opinion and in issue differences between Moral Majority supporters and their opponents. As Southern Baptist clergymen preach to more Southerners each week than do ministers of any other denomination, the views of this elite are potentially of considerable importance for public affairs. [6]

One long-term concern of both the Christian Right and the Christian Left has been social welfare policy. Moral Majority, Christian Voice, and the Religious Roundtable have clearly adopted the economic conservatism of secular New Right politicos. Is such conservatism widely shared among Southern Baptist ministers? Table 8.1 shows ministers' reactions to a widely used "federal role" question. Overall, Southern Baptist pastors reject the idea that the federal government should do more to solve social problems, although a large minority (almost 40 percent) feels such programs are desirable. The expected differences emerge among members, sympathizers, and opponents of Moral Majority. Results also hint that Rightists are more intense in their feelings, as they tend to disagree "strongly" with the statement, while supporters of a larger federal role merely "agree." Although this pattern is consistent throughout the survey, we should regard its meaning as suggestive only. A more sophisticated measure of intensity might not show the same result.

Despite the sizable minority of Southern Baptist ministers who would opt for a larger federal role in dealing with social problems, few pastors dissent from a statement that many government services should be performed instead by private enterprise. Indeed, the main difference between Christian Rightists and their opponents is in strength of agreement. Only about one-fourth of Moral Majority opponents reject this proposition. An even clearer example of consensus on private enterprise occurred when pastors were asked if oil companies should be owned by the federal government. Only a few ministers admit a preference for public ownership. Although the expected differences

TABLE 8.1

Issue Positions of Southern Baptist Ministers by Attitude toward Christian Right
(in percent)

Issue*	Ministers' Positions				
	Members	Sympathizers	Opponents	Have Not Heard	Total Sample
More federal effort to solve social problems					
Strongly agree	21	11	10	12	11
Agree	0	19	37	39	28
No opinion	14	5	6	6	6
Disagree	21	44	39	21	39
Strongly disagree	43	18	8	18	14
No answer	0	3	1	3	2
Total	99	100	101	99	100
Chi-square = p < .0001					
Gamma = -.24					
Government providing too many services					
Strongly agree	57	38	25	27	32
Agree	14	47	46	39	45
No opinion	7	5	8	18	8
Disagree	14	6	18	3	12
Strongly disagree	7	2	1	6	2
No answer	0	3	1	6	2
Total	99	101	99	99	100
Chi-square = p < .0001					
Gamma = .25					

Better if big oil owned by federal government

Strongly agree	7	3	3	6	4
Agree	7	4	6	6	5
No opinion	14	8	10	9	9
Disagree	21	40	50	36	44
Strongly disagree	50	44	31	39	38
No answer	0	2	1	3	2
Total	99	100	100	100	100

Chi-square = p > . 46
Gamma = -.15

Only free enterprise can be Christian

Strongly agree	71	32	23	27	29
Agree	21	40	38	33	38
No opinion	7	10	9	21	10
Disagree	0	12	24	15	17
Strongly disagree	0	2	6	0	3
No answer	0	5	1	3	3
Total	99	101	101	99	100

Chi-square = p < . 0002
Gamma = .21

Hard to be true Christian and liberal

Strongly agree	71	32	13	27	24
Agree	29	36	25	33	30
No opinion	0	11	13	15	12
Disagree	0	15	34	18	24
Strongly disagree	0	3	14	3	8
No answer	0	5	1	3	3
Total	99	102	100	99	101

Chi-square = p < . 0001
Gamma = .33

(continued)

TABLE 8.1 (continued)

Issue*	Members	Sympathizers	Ministers' Positions Opponents	Have Not Heard	Total Sample
United States should use force only when attacked					
Strongly agree	7	6	9	15	8
Agree	14	19	26	12	22
No opinion	14	6	8	21	9
Disagree	50	57	49	42	52
Strongly disagree	14	10	7	6	8
No answer	0	3	1	3	2
Total	99	101	100	99	101
Chi-square = p > .09					
Gamma = -.18					
United States should spend more on defense					
Strongly agree	79	44	15	18	29
Agree	14	44	48	52	45
No opinion	7	5	19	12	12
Disagree	0	5	17	6	11
Strongly disagree	0	1	2	3	1
No answer	0	3	1	9	2
Total	100	102	102	100	100
Chi-square = p < .0001					
Gamma = .48					
Carter made mistake pushing for SALT II					
Strongly agree	64	35	10	21	23
Agree	21	25	17	9	20
No opinion	7	14	17	18	16
Disagree	0	21	44	39	32

	(14)	(197)	(216)	(33)	(460)
Strongly disagree	7	3	10	6	7
No answer	0	3	2	6	3
Total	99	101	100	99	101
Chi-square = p < .0001					
Gamma = .44					
Congress should pass school prayer amendment					
Strongly agree	93	34	14	42	27
Agree	0	40	20	24	28
No opinion	7	5	5	9	5
Disagree	0	17	36	15	25
Strongly disagree	0	2	23	3	12
No answer	0	3	2	6	2
Total	100	101	100	99	99
Chi-square = p < .0001					
Gamma = .41					
Congress should pass abortion amendment					
Strongly agree	93	60	25	61	44
Agree	0	29	29	27	28
No opinion	7	2	4	6	3
Disagree	0	7	28	0	16
Strongly disagree	0	1	13	0	7
No answer	0	2	1	6	2
Total	100	101	100	100	100
Chi-square = p < .0001					
Gamma = .42					
(N)	(14)	(197)	(216)	(33)	(460)

*For complete wording of questionnaire items, see Appendix to Chapter 8.

Note: Percentages do not always total 100 because of rounding.

Source: Compiled by the author.

appear once more between Moral Majority sympathizers and opponents, they were not statistically significant.

The extent of ministerial support for free enterprise is also revealed in responses to a question designed to tap certain features of "civil religion." Pastors were asked whether "the free enterprise system is the only system which is really compatible with Christian beliefs." As such statements were a staple of Christian Right rhetoric during the 1980 campaign, it is not surprising that three-quarters of Moral Majority members and a third of sympathizers "agree strongly." Most of the remaining members and sympathizers simply "agree." More surprising, perhaps, even the Right's opponents provide substantial support for this claim. Evidently, many Baptist ministers automatically identify Christianity with capitalism, a connection that would have baffled saints of earlier ages.

A more divisive point is whether or not it is possible for a "true" Christian to be a political liberal. Both Moral Majority members and sympathizers overwhelmingly reject that possibility, while a plurality of their Southern Baptist opponents concede it. (Interestingly, Louis Harris discovered that a very large majority of laymen—including Evangelicals—see no religious disqualification in political liberalism. Perhaps Christian Right clergymen have a more rigid formulation of the nexus between Christian belief and political values than do most of their parishioners.)[7] In any case, the marriage of Christianity to conservative politics, which has so often troubled critics of civil religion, is made not only by the Christian Right but by a distressing number of more tolerant clerics as well.

Is the foreign-policy militarism of Jerry Falwell and other Christian Right leaders widely shared by Southern Baptist ministers? The answer is not simple. A majority of the ministers reject "attacking only when attacked" (something like a modern "just war" doctrine), although Christian Right opponents were slightly more likely to accept the notion. In addition, virtually three-quarters of the pastors support an increase in U.S. defense spending, including most opponents of Moral Majority (only 19 percent of whom oppose bigger military budgets). On the other hand SALT II found more support, having almost as many defenders as critics—including a majority among foes of the Christian Right. Internal lobbies such as the new Baptist Peacemakers organization might discover a ray of hope in this last finding. Southern Baptist ministers are apparently willing to negotiate mutual arms reduction but are unwilling to take unilateral action to either restrain defense spending or initiate reduction in nuclear arms. Perhaps they fall within the old religious tradition of Christian realism.

Two other issues that have agitated the SBC in recent years are school prayers and abortion. Until the 1982 annual meeting the SBC had steadfastly opposed efforts to reverse the Supreme Court's 1962 and 1963 decisions on religious exercises in public schools. But in 1982 Christian Right operatives won endorsement of a constitutional amendment allowing voluntary prayer. Similarly, the SBC has moved from a relatively moderate position on abortion to advocacy of right-to-life measures. [8] These issues clearly mark a division between the Right and its foes in our sample. An overwhelming majority of rightists favor the school prayer amendment, while a large majority of opponents reject it. And, while over two-thirds of the ministers support the Right on abortion, a substantial minority of antirightists oppose such an amendment. Obviously these two issues provide much of the tinder for political controversy within the SBC. In fact, a discriminant function analysis demonstrates that responses to the questions on school prayer, SALT II, and abortion are by far the most important in distinguishing Right and anti-Right ministers in the sample. [9]

Respondents were also asked whether laws regulating various forms of social behavior should be made stronger, weaker, or kept the same. About one-third of the ministers favor tougher gun controls, but big majorities advocate stronger laws on alcohol, pornography, and homosexuality. As previous studies have shown, even ministers who are liberal on most political issues tend to share conservative views on moral or so-called social-control questions. [10] Southern Baptists constitute no exception to that finding. It is somewhat curious to note, however, that the ministers are more likely to see the need for stronger laws on alcohol use than on homosexuality. Perhaps the Right's preoccupation with the latter issue has not had the impact of decades of Baptist attacks on "demon rum" (see Table 8.2).

To summarize the results and to facilitate further analysis, the ten questions in Table 8.1 were used to construct an index of political conservatism. Answers were coded from 1 ("strongly conservative") to 5 ("strongly liberal") and were combined in a simple additive index. The ministers' scores were then divided as closely as possible into quartiles. Table 8.3 shows the result of a crosstabulation between the index of policy conservatism and Moral Majority orientation. As Table 8.3 clearly indicates (perhaps better than the results on any single question), Moral Majority members are drawn from among the most consistently conservative ministers, while opponents fall more heavily into the liberal groups. (Keep in mind that these are relative categories. Very few of our "policy liberals" are self-identified political "liberals.")

Which ministers are most active politically? To answer that question another index was developed based on the frequency of participation in 14 political acts. Table 8.4 shows that the most conser-

TABLE 8.2

Positions of Southern Baptist Ministers on Current Social Legislation by Attitude toward Christian Right
(in percent)

| Issue* | Ministers' Positions | | | | |
	Members	Sympathizers	Opponents	Have Not Heard	Total Sample
Handgun ownership					
Stronger	14	28	43	42	36
As is	86	57	54	55	56
Weaker	0	12	2	0	6
No answer	0	2	1	3	2
Total	100	99	100	100	100

Chi-square = p < .0004
Gamma = -.24

	Members	Sympathizers	Opponents	Have Not Heard	Total Sample
Liquor sales to adults					
Stronger	100	87	77	85	83
As is	0	10	19	9	14
Weaker	0	1	1	3	1
No answer	0	2	2	3	2
Total	100	100	99	100	100

Chi-square = p > .1819
Gamma = .26

Sale of pornography					
Stronger	100	95	88	91	92
As is	0	2	11	3	6
Weaker	0	1	1	3	1
No answer	0	2	1	3	2
Total	100	100	101	100	101
Chi-square = p < .0355					
Gamma = .40					
Private homosexual acts					
Stronger	100	84	58	82	72
As is	0	12	36	6	23
Weaker	0	2	3	3	2
No answer	0	3	3	9	3
Total	100	101	100	100	100
Chi-square = p < .0001					
Gamma = .41					
(N)	(14)	(197)	(216)	(33)	(460)

*Respondents were asked if laws regulating the specified type of conduct should be made stronger, weaker, or kept about as they are.

Note: Percentages do not always total 100 because of rounding.

Source: Compiled by the author.

TABLE 8.3

Positions of Southern Baptist Ministers on Policy Conservatism/Liberalism Index by Attitude toward
Christian Right
(in percent)

	Ministers' Positions				
	Members	Sympathizers	Opponents	Have Not Heard	Total Sample
Ministers' position on index					
Most conservative	79	40	8	15	24
Conservative	14	28	16	30	22
Liberal	7	22	33	36	28
Most liberal	0	10	44	18	26
Total	100	100	101	99	100
(N)	(14)	(197)	(216)	(33)	(460)

Chi-square = $p < .0001$
Gamma = .55

Note: Percentages do not always total 100 because of rounding.

Source: Compiled by the author.

TABLE 8.4

Policy Conservatism and Levels of Activism of Southern Baptist Ministers
(in percent)

| | Ministers' Positions | | | | |
	Most Conservative	Conservative	Liberal	Most Liberal	Total Sample
Ministers' level of activism					
Very low	13	10	18	10	13
Low	18	29	32	24	25
Moderate	16	26	23	25	22
High	41	21	16	21	25
Very high	13	14	12	20	15
Total	101	100	101	100	100
(N)	(125)	(104)	(119)	(112)	(460)

Chi-square = p < .001

Note: Percentages do not always total 100 because of rounding.

Source: Compiled by the author.

vative ministers show up well in the "high" and "very high" activism categories, while the conservative group is concentrated in the "low" to "moderate" participation levels. Liberals are quite inactive, but the most liberal ministers have the largest proportion of any group in the "very high" category. Still, the overall advantage in activism is clearly with the conservatives.

What determines this pattern of activism? Drawing from findings in an earlier study that Moral Majority members and sympathizers had more positive attitudes toward activism than their opponents, we decided to test whether this is true of policy conservatives in the present study. A third index was constructed based on ministers' responses to 12 questions involving approval or disapproval of numerous types of clerical involvement. Again, the sample was divided into quartiles for analysis. Table 8.5 suggests that the most conservative ministers do dominate the "most positive" category, but that the most liberal ministers are not far behind. Indeed, the most liberal ministers have predominantly positive attitudes, while the two intermediate groups—but especially the liberals—tend to have more negative attitudes toward ministerial political involvement. Thus, in the realm of attitudes at least, ministers on the right and left ends of the Southern Baptist spectrum seem most favorably disposed toward political participation. This represents a substantial change from the 1960s and early 1970s when studies found liberal ministers much more likely than conservatives to approve of activism. [11]

Therefore, while disapproval of activism by some liberals may explain part of the conservative advantage, other factors must be considered. If earlier studies of clerical politics are correct, one restraint on liberal activism may be congregational resistance—especially feared by ministers in a denomination with conservative laymen and a congregational polity. To check this possibility an index was constructed based on ministers' answers to 12 questions asking how their congregations would react if they took various political actions ranging from urging a congregation to vote to committing civil disobedience. Table 8.6 reveals that perceived congregational support for ministerial politics declines as one moves from the most conservative to the liberal quartiles, with only a slight reversal of fortunes for the most liberal ministers. Quite probably, then, the conservative mood among Southern Baptist laymen has acted as a restraint on the political yearnings of moderate and liberal clergymen, while allowing many conservatives a freer hand.

How do various combinations of personal and congregational preferences affect ministerial activism? Table 8.7 summarizes the data. Conservatives considerably outnumber liberals in the most favorable situation for activism: where both minister and congregation approve of clerical activism. Liberals, on the other hand, dom-

TABLE 8.5

Policy Conservatism and Attitudes toward Activism of Southern Baptist Ministers
(in percent)

	Ministers' Positions				
	Most Conservative	Conservative	Liberal	Most Liberal	Total Sample
Ministers' attitudes toward activism					
Most positive	38	30	12	31	28
Positive	24	23	20	33	25
Negative	17	26	33	21	24
Most negative	22	21	35	15	24
Total	101	100	100	100	101
(N)	(125)	(104)	(119)	(112)	(460)

Chi-square = p < .0001

Note: Percentages do not always total 100 because of rounding.

Source: Compiled by the author.

TABLE 8.6

Congregational Attitudes toward Activism and Policy Conservatism of Southern Baptist Ministers
(in percent)

	Ministers' Positions				
	Most Conservative	Conservative	Liberal	Most Liberal	Total Sample
Congregations' attitude toward activism					
Very positive	30	22	13	13	19
Positive	21	21	16	20	19
Uncertain	22	23	19	26	22
Negative	14	17	23	22	19
Very negative	14	16	20	20	20
Total	101	99	101	101	100
(N)	(125)	(104)	(119)	(112)	(460)

Chi-square = $p < .006$

Note: Percentages do not always total 100 because of rounding.

Source: Compiled by the author.

176

inate combinations where either the minister, the church, or both
are negative toward ministerial involvement. But Table 8.7 also
shows that these factors together do not explain all the conservative
advantage. Even when conservative and liberal ministers exhibit the
same attitudes toward activism and are placed in similar congregational environments, they often participate at different rates. Where
minister and church approve of activism, 65 percent of both liberals
and conservatives are highly active. And where both minister and
church reject involvement, only 16 percent of the conservatives and
15 percent of the liberals participate. In the mixed categories, however, conservatives surpass their liberal counterparts. Whether
this is due to conservatives' more intense feeling about issues or due
to the Right's superior machinery for mobilization, one cannot tell.

Where do the conservative ministerial politicos come from?
As might be expected, a number of theological, political, personal,
and organizational variables are associated with policy conservatism
among Southern Baptist ministers. We can do no more than note
some of the correlates of conservatism. As shown in Table 8.8,
policy conservatism is especially prevalent among Fundamentalists,
Republicans, Reagan voters, self-identified political conservatives,
and those moving toward the GOP in recent years. In socioeconomic
terms policy conservatism is found most frequently among ministers
with farm, blue-collar, and business backgrounds; relatively modest
educations; and training at the more conservative Southern Baptist
(and non-Southern Baptist) seminaries. They are likely to be 29 years
of age and under, or 70 years of age and older. The predominance of
conservatives among the young reflects the much-noted selective re-
cruitment of theological and political conservatives into the ministry
in recent years, while the strong showing of conservatives among
ministers over age 60 results in large part from the modest social
and educational background of ministers in that age group. [12]

The organizational location of conservatives is also intriguing.
They are situated disproportionately in small- to medium-sized
churches and in the Deep South and Southwest, while larger churches
and those in the South Atlantic region are the homes of the liberals.
Working-class churches seem to harbor conservatives, while both
lower-middle-class and upper-middle-class churches favor liberals.
Policy conservatives also seem somewhat marginal to the organizational
life of the denomination, predominating among pastors who have never
attended a Southern Baptist Convention and among those who have
served only briefly in their current position. These lines of division
on recent political controversies correspond in striking fashion to several historical cleavages within the Southern Baptist Convention. [13]

What do these findings suggest about future ministerial politics
among Southern Baptists? The picture at present is quite confusing.

TABLE 8.7

Positions of Conservative and Liberal Ministers by Ministerial and Congregational Attitudes toward Activism
(in percent)

	Minister and Church Attitudes[a]					
	Positive Positive	Positive Unclear	Positive Negative	Negative Positive	Negative Unclear	Negative Negative
Policy attitudes of ministers						
Conservative[b]	64	56	33	51	44	42
Liberal[b]	36	44	67	49	56	58
Total	100	100	100	100	100	100
(N)	(129)	(52)	(61)	(49)	(50)	(119)
Proportion of active ministers by situation[c]						
Conservative	65	69	50	24	27	16
Liberal	65	52	42	25	14	15

[a]Top column headings indicate ministerial attitudes toward activism; bottom column headings indicate congregational attitudes toward ministerial activism.

[b]"Conservative" and "liberal" categories are collapsed from the four categories in Table 8.3.

[c]Percentages represent the proportion of ministers in each cell who score "high" or "very high" on the activism index used in Table 8.4. Thus 65 percent of the conservatives who approve of activism and have supportive churches actually participate at a high level.

Source: Compiled by the author.

TABLE 8.8

Policy Conservatism of Southern Baptist Ministers by
Theological, Political, and Personal Background Variables
(in percent)

Variable	Policy Conservative
Theology	
Fundamentalist	64
Conservative	48
Moderate	15
Liberal	0
Political party	
Republican	65
Democratic	37
Independent	42
Other	48
Recent party movement	
More Republican	62
More Democratic	12
More Independent	48
Not moved	40
Self-identified political philosophy	
Conservative	60
Moderate	15
Liberal	0
1980 presidential vote	
Reagan	66
Carter	22
Father's occupation	
Farmer	46
Blue collar	51
Clerical	39
Minister	44
Professional	32
Business	47
Secular education	
Grade school	67
High school	56
Some college	57
College degree	44
Postgraduate work	52
Seminary education	
None	58
Some seminary	47
Seminary graduate	46
Postgraduate work	39

(continued)

TABLE 8.8 (continued)

Variable	Policy Conservative
Seminary attended	
Southern	26
Southeastern	27
Midwestern and Golden Gate	38
Southwestern	50
New Orleans	56
Fundamentalist	66
Age	
29 or under	60
30–39	47
40–49	45
50–59	46
60–69	54
70 or over	90
Region of residence	
Southwest	62
Deep and Mid-South	50
Midwest and Northeast	42
Pacific Coast	42
South Atlantic	34
Size of present church (members)	
1–99	49
100–99	47
200–99	54
300–499	54
500–999	36
1,000 and over	34
Class of church	
Working class	53
Mixed	49
Lower middle class	41
Upper middle class	33
Attendance at SBC convention (times)	
Never	57
1–2	42
3–5	48
6 or more	40
Years at present church	
Less than 1	55
1–2	45
3–4	54
5–10	43
11 or more	38

Source: Compiled by the author.

Although Southern Baptist ministers are deeply ambivalent about organizations such as Moral Majority, they are clearly in the conservative camp on most issues. Still, on some questions a substantial minority with more moderate or even liberal views appears. At first glance it might seem this minority is sure to grow: the ministers are drawn from middle-class backgrounds, have both college and seminary degrees, and serve the burgeoning middle-class, urban contingent within the SBC. The increasing numbers of such ministers and congregations would seem to provide the basis for a strong moderate-to-liberal faction.

However, there are clear countervailing tendencies. The shift in the Southern Baptist center of gravity from the South Atlantic states to the Deep South and Southwest continues and will strengthen the hand of conservatives. (The last three SBC presidents have come from these areas.) In a related vein, conservative seminaries in the same regions have grown most rapidly, producing added numbers of ministerial conservatives. And new ministers everywhere are predominantly conservative, augmenting the potential for Christian Right politics. These conflicting forces, combined with increased activism by the most conservative and the most liberal ministers alike, point toward increasing politicization and polarization within the denomination. Thus the Southern Baptist Convention, like the South itself, may be seeing the rise of two-party politics. The battles of the past few years may just be skirmishes preliminary to a much longer war.

APPENDIX TO CHAPTER 8

Questions Used for Issue Analysis

Please indicate how strongly you agree or disagree:

The federal government should do more to solve social problems such as poverty, unemployment, and poor housing.

The government is providing too many services that should be left to private enterprise.

It would be better if the big oil companies were owned by the federal government.

The free enterprise system is the only system that is really compatible with Christian beliefs.

It would be hard to be both a true Christian and a political liberal.

The United States should use its military forces only when it is attacked.

The United States should spend more money for the military and defense.

President Carter made a mistake pushing for a strategic arms limitation treaty with the Russians.

Congress should quickly pass a constitutional amendment that would permit prayer as a regular exercise in all public schools.

Congress should quickly pass a constitutional amendment prohibiting all abortions, unless necessary to save the mother's life.

NOTES

1. Richard Marius, "The War between the Baptists," Esquire 96 (December 1981): 46-55.

2. For earlier works on clerical politics, see Jeffrey K. Hadden, The Gathering Storm in the Churches (Garden City, N. Y.: Anchor, 1970); and Harold Quinley, The Prophetic Clergy (New York: Wiley & Sons, 1974).

3. For response rates in other studies of ministers, see Hadden, Gathering Storm, p. 42; Quinley, The Prophetic Clergy, pp. 316-17; and Research and Forecasts, Inc., The Connecticut Mutual Report on American Values in the '80s: The Impact of Belief (Hartford: Connecticut Mutual Life Insurance Company, 1981), p. 275.

4. James L. Guth, "The Southern Baptist Clergy: Vanguard of the Christian Right?" in The New Christian Right: Mobilization and Legitimation, ed. Robert Liebman and Robert Wuthnow (Hawthorne, N. Y.: Aldine, 1983).

5. James L. Guth, "The Politics of Preachers: Southern Baptist Ministers and the Christian Right" (Paper presented at the 1982 Citadel Symposium on Southern Politics, Charleston, S. C., March 25-27, 1982). This paper appears in abbreviated form in David G. Bromley and Anson Shupe, eds., New Christian Politics (Macon, Ga.: Mercer University Press, 1983).

6. Although the Southern Baptist Convention is increasingly a national organization, its base is still in the South and border states. Well over three-quarters of the ministers in our sample are presently serving churches in these areas. Over 90 percent are pastors of southern churches or are themselves of predominantly southern origins.

7. Harris's finding is cited in Seymour Martin Lipset and Earl Raab, "The Election and the Evangelicals," Commentary 71 (March 1981): 25-31.

8. Charles Austin, "Southern Baptists Back Constitution Amendment on School Prayer," New York Times, June 18, 1982, p. 12. See also Stan Hasty, "McAteer Key Figure in SBC Swing to the Right," Baptist Public Affairs, July 8, 1982.

9. The standardized canonical discriminant function coefficients for school prayer, SALT II, and abortion were .410, .346, and .345, respectively. Military spending came in a poor fourth at .258.

10. Quinley, The Prophetic Clergy, pp. 64-70.

11. Ibid., pp. 136-56.

12. For analysis of the changing face of the American clergy, see Haddon Robinson, "A Profile of the American Clergyman," Christianity Today 24 (May 23, 1980): 27-29.

13. James J. Thompson, Jr., Tried as by Fire: Southern Baptists and the Religious Controversies of the 1920s (Macon, Ga.: Mercer University Press, 1982).

9

CONCLUSION: THE RELIGIOUS FACTOR IN CONTEMPORARY SOUTHERN POLITICS

Laurence W. Moreland
Robert P. Steed
Tod A. Baker

Scholarly literature on the South over the past half-century has tended to argue two potentially contradictory themes. The first and older theme has depicted the South's uniqueness, emphasizing the cultural differences that have furnished fertile ground for images of the South so often depicted in fiction. This theme has had many variants, with observers remarking upon a variety of clusters of southern attitudes and behaviors that have been identified as constituting the basis for the idea of southern distinctiveness. As many of the chapters in this volume have noted, Fundamentalist or Evangelical Protestantism[1] has often been identified not just as an element of southern distinctiveness but as one of its primary and unifying characteristics.[2]

The second and newer theme is one of a South immersed in change: a region that is rapidly industrializing and urbanizing; that is adapting its traditional social structure, especially with regard to race, to the legal and social imperatives of the day; and that is absorbing, along with the Southwest, an influx of nonnatives who see the country's future as centered in the newly emergent Sun Belt. This theme concentrates on the mushrooming data that seem to certify the long-awaited emergence of the New South, often characterized as a region finally nationalized in its social, economic, and political life, yet providing the kind of opportunities no longer so available in the older, industrialized regions of the nation. In this context the politics of the South has received special attention, and changes in southern political life have been extensively documented.[3]

These two themes, the persistence of the old and the emergence of the new, would appear to be on a collision course: the more the latter characterizes the region, the less the former can logically retain its descriptive and explanatory power. Thus one might expect, for example, that to the extent that this is the case the impact of

Fundamentalist religion on politics should be of negligible or of decreasing proportions by the 1980s. Yet, in fact, one of the most notable political phenomena of the 1980 presidential election was the emergence of the New Christian Right, a phenomenon thought to be especially noteworthy in the South. How, then, can this seeming inconsistency be explained? The answer may lie paradoxically in the conclusion that both themes simultaneously contain substantial degrees of truth. As Michael Mezey observed in Chapter 1, there is not one South, but many Souths; the forces of change have advanced far in some ways, but in other ways the region's traditions remain strong. Racially, geographically, economically, politically, and socially, the South is a mixture of subgroups that behave with varying degrees of consistency with historically dominant, traditional cultural patterns, thus creating complexities requiring careful and cautious analysis. This general observation applies to southern religion as well.

The research reported in this volume has tended on the whole to demonstrate the lessened contemporary impact of religion on southern politics. Certainly the studies show that religion is relevant, though not crucial, to understanding the region's political behavior. At the mass level of political participation (Part I of this volume) Michael Mezey found in Chapter 1 that Southerners are different from non-Southerners on only some points, such as attitudes toward race and some moral issues, and not at all different on others, such as attitudes on economic issues and the role of government. He did find differences with respect to religion; although these differences are generally modest, they are strongest for rural, lower-income whites. In Chapter 2 Corwin Smidt addressed the task of identifying those Southerners that fall within the historically important group known as Evangelicals. He found that although the proportion of Evangelicals is more than twice as great in the South as in the non-South, they nevertheless constitute less than one-third of the entire southern population. Furthermore, even among white Evangelicals, less than 40 percent of his sample characterize themselves as politically conservative. Even then, that conservatism is primarily a moral conservatism, not the economic individualism of secular conservatives. Consistent with Mezey's analysis, Smidt found Evangelicals to be older, less educated, and more likely to live in rural areas and small towns than non-Evangelicals.

In Chapter 3 Jerry Perkins, Donald Fairchild, and Murray Havens, examining the impact of religion on race, found that the proportion of Evangelicals among blacks is nearly twice as great as among whites. While the social characteristics and attitudinal orientations of both white and black Evangelicals are often similar, they nevertheless do not constitute a unified political force. For blacks the racial experience appears to be dominant; as a consequence, one

may continue to expect that the kinds of appeals likely to be attractive
to white Evangelicals—appeals with a high moral content like those
relating to abortion and the family in general—will probably not mobilize black voters, whether Evangelical or not. Therefore, analysis
of the political behavior of Evangelicals in the South must recognize
that a large portion of them are black, and that that group is simply
not likely to respond to the issues that have in the past few years mobilized the New Christian Right.

Kenneth Wald and Michael Lupfer sought in Chapter 4 to link
religious conviction to actual political behavior. Their findings cast
further doubt that a religious Right can wield decisive political power
in the South. In focusing on what they identify as the religiously orthodox (an essentially Evangelical group) in one southern urban area,
they concluded that religious orthodoxy influences political behavior
"only in the absence of countervailing factors." In 1980 Republican
attempts to attract religious Fundamentalists in eastern Tennessee
were largely frustrated by the long-time, strong Democratic identification of older, less-educated, lower-economic-status whites (the
very group to which conservative Republican issues would seem to be
directed) and by Jimmy Carter's own well-publicized born-again experience. Like the other research reported in Part I concerning
mass attitudes and behavior, the Wald-Lupfer study found that religious appeals would most likely mobilize Evangelical voters when
those appeals are couched in moral terms; other issues attractive to
secular conservatives, such as a balanced budget, appear to be much
less likely to lure Evangelical voters into conservative Republican
politics.

The research reported in Part II examined the links between
religion and political elites and between politics and religious elites.
Robert P. Steed, Laurence W. Moreland, and Tod A. Baker noted in
Chapter 5 that religious Fundamentalists among southern political activists differ little from their non-Fundamentalist fellow activists on
personal and political background characteristics. In addition, while
southern Fundamentalist activists are certainly more conservative
than nonsouthern Fundamentalist activists, so too are southern non-
Fundamentalist activists more conservative than nonsouthern non-
Fundamentalists. In the context of different regional party systems,
the authors concluded that Fundamentalism in the South, at least with
regard to political activists, has its effect primarily in that larger
and more active numbers of Fundamentalists are represented in the
political elite there than in nonsouthern political elites.

Tod Baker, Robert P. Steed, and Laurence W. Moreland found
in Chapter 6 that what is true of southern whites in the mass electorate
(as documented in Part I) is also true of southern political activists:
that is, issues with a moral content tend to differentiate southern

Fundamentalist activists from non-Fundamentalist activists. In other words, to the extent that Fundamentalism describes distinctive southern viewpoints, it does so only in that one issue area. In other issue areas race and party identification tend to play much more important roles in differentiating activists who are Fundamentalist from activists who are not.

In Chapter 7 Alan Abramowitz, John McGlennon, and Ronald Rapoport observed that Fundamentalists newly active in partisan politics can be remarkably opportunistic. The authors present as an example the Fundamentalists in Virginia who participated in the 1978 Democratic senatorial nominating convention in support of a specific candidacy, who then shifted significantly to the Republican party in voting in the 1978 general election (their candidate having failed to obtain the Democratic nomination for U.S. Senator), and who finally in 1980 became generally active in the Republican party as well as in the Democratic party. At least for relatively newly active Fundamentalists (who are responding perhaps to moral issues in the main), the Virginia experience suggests that they have some capacity for disrupting or distorting the regularity of party politics as well as for influencing the party system in a generally conservative direction.

In a study of the clerical elite (ministers) within the Southern Baptist Convention, James Guth concluded in Chapter 8 that, like the contemporary South in general, the Southern Baptist clergy does not constitute a monolithic entity. While most Southern Baptist ministers are self-described as politically conservative, about one-half do not approve of organizations such as Moral Majority; in addition, there are considerable differences on attitudes toward specific issues although the conservative view generally prevails among a majority of the ministers. Despite these differences, the actual political behavior of the ministers suggests a somewhat different picture. Although the politically most liberal ministers are just as likely as the politically most conservative ministers to be highly positive in their attitudes toward political activism on the part of Southern Baptist clergy, the fact remains that the most conservative ministers are significantly more likely to be activist in the political realm.

Taken collectively, the research reported in this volume tells a great deal about the current state of religion and politics in the South. At the outset, it is apparent that it is possible to both overestimate and underestimate the impact of religion on southern politics. Treatment of the Christian Right in the popular media with regard to the 1980 elections might make Evangelical or Fundamentalist religion seem to be a new and ineluctable force in U.S., especially southern, politics. Yet our conclusion here can only be that its influence has been exaggerated. Only a minority proportion of the southern electorate can be classified as Evangelical or Fundamentalist; even among

white Evangelicals or Fundamentalists only a minority identify themselves as conservative. Furthermore, southern white politically
conservative Evangelical or Fundamentalist voters respond as an
identifiable political group to primarily one vein of contemporary
conservatism: issues tapping a moral dimension rather than economic
or defense dimensions. Still further, the presence of countervailing
forces such as strong (Democratic) party identification may addition-
ally impede the mobilization of conservative southern religionists.
Finally, southern Evangelicals or Fundamentalists who are black—
and who make up a substantial portion of southern Evangelicals and
Fundamentalists—are much more likely to respond to appeals based
on racial overtures (often translated into economic terms) rather than
religious overtures.

In the light of these data, how can we explain the appearance of
the prominence of religion in southern politics in recent years? A
partial explanation may lie in the chapters in this volume on elites,
the most visible segment of the population. Evangelicals and Fundamentalists are not only more numerous in the general population in
the South than in the non-South but are more numerous among the
southern political elite as well; just as important, southern Fundamentalist activists appear to have higher levels of activity than nonsouthern Fundamentalist activists. A similar observation about the
Southern Baptist clergy buttresses this point: the most conservative
Southern Baptist ministers are also the most active. Finally, it may
well be that the attempts of the New Christian Right leadership to define the political agenda in their own terms received more media attention than their actual success in mobilizing the electorate.

Despite these findings, we should not underestimate the impact
—real or potential—of conservative religion on southern politics.
Electoral success typically depends upon building coalitions among
voters by adding increment to increment until a majority is obtained.
Fundamentalist voters in the South constitute a very large increment,
and if they can be mobilized as a cohesive voting group (this is a very
large "if"), their political potential will be great.

The research reported in this volume does not necessarily question earlier research arguing that conservative religion is an important distinguishing element of southern distinctiveness. First, the
earlier research employed methods and data different from those
utilized by the studies presented in this volume, and that may account
for at least some of the differences.[4] Second, it may well be that
although conservative religion is in some ways distinctive to southern
culture,[5] it has not necessarily been directly related to southern electoral behavior.[6] If this is the case, perhaps our findings of limited
religious impact on southern electoral politics are not inconsistent
with earlier research demonstrating a broader and more subtle influ-

ence on southern culture as a whole. Third, perhaps the southern political agenda has changed. As noted in much of the research in this volume, Fundamentalists and Evangelicals are most likely to respond as a political group to issues with substantial moral content. During the long period (extending roughly to the mid-1960s) when southern politics was preeminently the politics of race, the political agenda was indeed one of moral content, for the racial segregation issue was typically framed by white supremacists in moral terms and the structure of the region's racial relations was typically seen as divinely inspired.[7] As the race issue has receded, at least in terms of overt white-supremacist appeals, that kind of moral element has disappeared from southern politics to be replaced by economic and other kinds of political issues.[8] Finally, it may well be that southern Fundamentalists and Evangelicals themselves have changed. As Samuel Hill observed in the introduction to this volume, the South has been increasingly drawn into the nation's mainstream for a variety of reasons—the impact of national legal imperatives such as the Brown v. Board of Education decision in 1954 and the Voting Rights Act of 1965, of the homogenization of the nation's culture promoted by television and other media, of the influx into the South of large numbers of nonnatives, of the urbanization and industrialization of the South, among other causes—and therefore southern religion, while different, may not be as different or as politically important as it once was.[9]

Conservative religion in the South continues to be a characteristic of southern distinctiveness, to the extent that that distinctiveness survives. But its potential impact on the political system appears to be limited to issues raising clear (and often traditional) moral dimensions: abortion, gambling, liquor control, and so forth. In the absence of those issues, Fundamentalists and Evangelicals will behave politically along lines related to factors other than religion, and the impact of religion will continue to remain confined to a more general and diffused influence on the larger regional culture. However, the potential for impact on southern electoral politics remains: if the southern, or national, political agenda were to be effectively redefined in primarily moralistic terms, the role of religion might become more important, if not decisive, both for the South and for the nation.

NOTES

1. As several chapters point out, there are technical definitional distinctions among terms such as Fundamentalism, Evangelicalism, and religious orthodoxy. Since the general thrust of this volume is more toward exploring the broad linkages between religion and southern politics than toward clarifying the semantic and theo-

logical details involved in these terms, we choose to concentrate on their points of basic commonality (for example, acceptance of the Bible as the literal word of God) and to use them pretty much interchangeably. In this chapter we follow this practice except in the chapter summaries and related references where terminology used by the respective authors is utilized.

2. See, for example, the extended discussions of southern distinctiveness in Chapters 1 and 6 of this volume.

3. A large body of literature addresses the changes that have taken place in the South since World War II. Among the more useful materials are John C. McKinney and Edgar T. Thompson, eds., The South in Continuity and Change (Durham, N.C.: Duke University Press, 1965); Avery Leiserson, ed., The American South in the 1960's (New York: Praeger, 1964); Samuel D. Cook, "Political Movements and Organizations," Journal of Politics 26 (February 1964): 130-53; Allan P. Sindler, ed., Change in the Contemporary South (Durham, N.C.: Duke University Press, 1963); Bernard Cosman, Five States for Goldwater (University: University of Alabama Press, 1966); Donald S. Strong, "Further Reflections on Southern Politics," Journal of Politics 33 (May 1971): 239-56; James L. Sundquist, Dynamics of the Party System: Alignment and Realignment of Political Parties in the United States (Washington, D.C.: Brookings Institution, 1973), pp. 245-74; Numan V. Bartley and Hugh D. Graham, Southern Politics and the Second Reconstruction (Baltimore: Johns Hopkins University Press, 1975); William C. Havard, ed., The Changing Politics of the South (Baton Rouge: Louisiana State University Press, 1972), especially chap. 1; Jack Bass and Walter DeVries, The Transformation of Southern Politics (New York: Basic Books, 1976); Earl Black, Southern Governors and Civil Rights (Cambridge, Mass.: Harvard University Press, 1976); Bruce A. Campbell, "Change in the Southern Electorate," American Journal of Political Science 21 (February 1977): 37-64; Paul Allen Beck, "Partisan Realignment in the Postwar South," American Political Science Review 71 (June 1977): 477-96; Louis M. Seagull, Southern Republicanism (New York: Schenkman, 1975); Alan I. Abramowitz, "Ideological Realignment and the Nationalization of Southern Politics: A Study of Party Activists and Candidates in a Southern State" (Paper presented at the 1979 Annual Meeting of the Southern Political Science Association, Gatlinburg, Tenn., November 1-3, 1979); and Robert P. Steed, Laurence W. Moreland, and Tod A. Baker, eds., Party Politics in the South (New York: Praeger, 1980), especially Introduction by William C. Havard.

4. Historical studies, for example, have normally not used quantitative data. See, among others, William B. Hesseltine, The South in American History (Englewood Cliffs, N.J.: Prentice-Hall, 1936).

5. See John Shelton Reed, The Enduring South: Subcultural Persistence in a Mass Society (Lexington, Mass.: D. C. Heath, Lexington Books, 1972).

6. See Samuel S. Hill's discussion in the introduction to this volume.

7. On the centrality of race in traditional southern politics, see V. O. Key, Jr., Southern Politics in State and Nation (New York: Alfred A. Knopf, 1949).

8. Refer to the discussion in Earl Black, "Southern Governors and Political Change: Campaign Stances on Racial Segregation and Economic Development, 1950-1969," Journal of Politics 33 (August 1971): 703-34.

9. Bass and DeVries, The Transformation of Southern Politics, especially chap. 1.

ABOUT THE EDITORS AND CONTRIBUTORS

TOD A. BAKER (Ph.D., University of Tennessee) is professor of political science at The Citadel. A codirector of The Citadel Symposium on Southern Politics, he has coedited two books, Party Politics in the South (1980) and Contemporary Southern Political Attitudes and Behavior (1982). He is author or coauthor of a number of professional papers and has published in the areas of urban politics, party activists, political socialization, and South Carolina politics.

ROBERT P. STEED (Ph.D., University of Virginia) is professor of political science at The Citadel. A codirector of The Citadel Symposium on Southern Politics, he has coedited two books, Party Politics in the South (1980) and Contemporary Southern Political Attitudes and Behavior (1982). He has done substantial research and publication in the areas of party activists, the presidency, political socialization, and South Carolina politics. He is currently working on a book on contemporary political issues.

LAURENCE W. MORELAND (M.A., Duke University) is associate professor of political science at The Citadel. He is codirector of The Citadel Symposium on Southern Politics and has coedited two books, Party Politics in the South (1980) and Contemporary Southern Political Attitudes and Behavior (1982). He has coauthored a number of publications and professional papers and is currently involved in research for a book on contemporary political issues.

ALAN ABRAMOWITZ (Ph.D., Stanford University) is associate professor of political science at the State University of New York at Stony Brook. He has published in numerous professional journals and has contributed chapters to three recently published books. His research interests focus on party leadership and party realignment in the South. He is currently editing a manuscript for a book-length study of party activists.

DONALD FAIRCHILD (Ph.D., University of California at Los Angeles) is professor of political science at Georgia State University. He has served as consultant to a variety of governmental agencies and has published several articles on Georgia politics.

JAMES L. GUTH (Ph.D., Harvard University) is associate professor of political science at Furman University. He is author of more than two dozen publications and professional papers. He has done extensive research and publication in the areas of religion and politics. His other research interests include agricultural policies and politics and the legislative process.

MURRAY HAVENS (Ph.D., Johns Hopkins University) is professor of political science at Texas Tech University. He is author of four books and numerous journal articles and professional papers. He is currently serving as book review editor for the Journal of Politics.

SAMUEL S. HILL (Ph.D., Duke University) is professor of religion at the University of Florida. He is probably the leading authority on religion in the South. His books include The New Religious-Political Right in America (1982), The South and the North in American Religion (1980), Religion and the Solid South (1972), and Southern Churches in Crisis (1967).

MICHAEL LUPFER (Ph.D., University of Miami) is professor of psychology at Memphis State University. He is author of ten professional papers and fifteen articles. He has published in journals such as Journal of Psychology, Journal of Politics, Journal of Conflict Resolution, and Social Science Quarterly.

JOHN MCGLENNON (Ph.D., Johns Hopkins University) is assistant professor of government at the College of William and Mary. His publications include work on police bureaucracy and state party activists. He is currently engaged in research on police corruption and state party leaders; he is also editing a book-length manuscript on state party activists. In 1982 he was a candidate for the U.S. House of Representatives from Virginia.

MICHAEL L. MEZEY (Ph.D., Syracuse University) is professor of political science at DePaul University. His book Comparative Legislatures was published in 1979. He has published in numerous professional journals such as Journal of Politics, Public Opinion Quarterly, and Western Political Quarterly. He is author of 20 papers presented at a number of leading professional conferences.

JERRY PERKINS (Ph.D., Emory University) is associate professor of political science at Texas Tech University; during the 1982-83 academic year he served as visiting associate professor at the University of Miami. He has published articles in numerous professional journals including American Political Science Review.

RONALD B. RAPOPORT (Ph.D., University of Michigan) is assistant professor of government at the College of William and Mary. He has published articles in a number of professional journals; most recently his research interests have focused on state party activists.

CORWIN SMIDT (Ph.D., University of Iowa) is associate professor of political science at Calvin College. His research interests include public opinion and voting behavior as well as religion and politics. He has published numerous articles in journals such as Sociological Analysis, Political Behavior, and American Politics Quarterly. He has presented papers at a number of professional conferences and meetings.

KENNETH WALD (Ph.D., Washington University) is associate professor of political science at the University of Florida. He is author of two books and ten journal articles. His research interests include British voting patterns, presidential debates, and the Ku Klux Klan as well as religion and politics.